The Basics of Astrology—Explained

Now for the first time you can learn the basics of astrology in one, easy-to-read book. *Astrology for Beginners* explains all of the essentials including planets, houses, aspects, chart construction, interpretation and much more.

- *Learn what astrology is and what it can do for you*
- *Create and interpret your natal (birth) chart*
- *Explore transits, predictive astrology and progressions*
- *Calculate a precisely accurate horoscope chart*
- *Learn about references for more detailed material*

Astrology for Beginners begins by presenting the philosophy of astrology and then gives you simple definitions of its terms. This book bridges the gap of the language of astrology and provides you with the tools needed to explore all of the astrological details.

Author William Hewitt explains each Sun Sign with simplicity and accuracy in an easy-to-understand manner. He includes the three different methods for constructing your chart—the modern way, the fast way, and the original way—and gives a detailed description of each.

In every case this book is simple and clear. Many descriptions are supported with illustrated examples including Hewitt's own natal chart.

With *Astrology for Beginners* you will learn all of the fundamentals of the amazing science of astrology!

About the Author

William W. Hewitt has been practicing astrology professionally, as an avocation, since early 1974. He is a member of the American Federation of Astrologers and specializes in natal charts and interpretation. Hewitt has also been a professional clinical hypnotist since 1972. He has his own practice in Colorado where he resides. A member of the National Writer's Club, Hewitt lectures on various subjects including astrology, hypnosis, psychic phenomena, mind control, and other areas. He is the author of *Hypnosis*, *Beyond Hypnosis*, and *Tea Leaf Reading*.

To Write to the Author

If you wish to contact the author or would like more information about this book, please write to the author in care of Llewellyn Worldwide, and we will forward your request. Both the author and publisher appreciate hearing from you and learning of your enjoyment of this book and how it has helped you. Llewellyn Worldwide cannot guarantee that every letter written to the author can be answered, but all will be forwarded. Please write to:

Llewellyn's New Worlds of Mind and Spirit
P.O. Box 64383 Dept. L307-8
St. Paul, MN 55164-0383, U.S.A.

Please enclose a self-addressed, stamped envelope for reply, or $1.00 to cover costs. If outside the U.S.A., enclose international postal reply coupon.

Llewellyn's Modern Astrology Library

Astrology For Beginners

An Easy Guide to Understanding and Interpreting Your Chart

William W. Hewitt

1998
Llewellyn Publications
St. Paul, Minnesota 55164-0383, U.S.A.

FIRST EDITION
Eighth Printing, 1998

Cover design by Christopher Wells

Library of Congress Cataloging-in-Publication Data
Hewitt, William W., 1929–
    Astrology for beginners: an easy guide to understanding and interpreting your chart / by William W. Hewitt.
    p.   cm. — (Llewellyn's modern astrology library series)
    Includes bibliographical references.
    ISBN 0-87542-307-8
    1. Astrology. I. Title. II. Series.
BF1708.1.H48   1992
133.5—dc20   91-36399
                                                        CIP

Publisher's note:
Llewellyn Worldwide does not participate in, endorse, or have any authority or responsibility concerning private business transactions between our authors and the public.
    All mail addressed to the author is forwarded but the publisher cannot, unless specifically instructed by the author, give out an address or phone number.

Printed in the United States of America

Llewellyn Publications
A Division of Llewellyn Worldwide, Ltd.
P.O. 64383, St. Paul, MN 55164-0383

About the Llewellyn Modern Astrology Library

The books in this series are on the leading edge of practical and applied astrology as we move toward the culmination of the 20th century.

This is not speculative astrology, nor astrology so esoteric as to have little practical application in meeting the needs of people in these critical times. Yet, these books go far beyond the meaning of "practicality" as seen prior to the 1990s. Our needs are spiritual as well as mundane, planetary as well as particular, evolutionary as well as progressive. Astrology grows with the times, and our times make heavy demands upon Intelligence and Wisdom.

The authors are all professional astrologers drawing from their own practice and knowledge of historical persons and events, demonstrating proof of their conclusions with the horoscopes of real people in real situations.

Modern Astrology relates the individual person to the Universe in which he/she lives, not as a passive victim of alien forces but as an active participant in an environment expanded to the breadth and depth of the Cosmos. We are not alone, and our responsibilities are infinite.

The horoscope is both a measure and a guide to personal movement—seeing every act undertaken, every decision made, every event as *time dynamic:* with effects that move through the many dimensions of space and levels of consciousness in fulfillment of Will and Purpose. Every act becomes an act of Will, for we extend our awareness to consequences reaching to the ends of time and space.

This is astrology supremely important to this unique period in human history, when Pluto transits through Scorpio and Neptune through Capricorn. The books in this series are intended to provide insight into the critical needs and the critical decisions that must be made.

These books, too, are "active agents," bringing to the reader knowledge which will liberate the higher forces inside each person to the end that we may fulfill that for which we were intended.

— Carl Llewellyn Weschcke

Other Books by William Hewitt

Hypnosis
Tea Leaf Reading
Bridges to Success & Fulfillment
The Art of Self Talk
Psychic Development for Beginners
Hypnosis for Beginners
Self-Hypnosis for a Better Life

Audio Tapes

Become Smoke-Free through Self-Hypnosis
Psychic Workout through Self-Hypnosis
Relaxation and Stress Management through Self-Hypnosis
Your Perfect Weight through Self-Hypnosis

*This book is dedicated to
my wife, Dolores, who is the
Sun and the Stars in my life.*

ACKNOWLEDGEMENTS

The following portions of this book are reprinted by the kind permission of *Horoscope Guide*, JBH Publishing Company, Inc.:

Chapter 2. From *Horoscope Guide* May 1988, article "Meeting The Challenge" by William W. Hewitt.

Chapter 4. From *Horoscope Guide*'s 1987 Astro Annual, article "Mini–Profiles" by William W. Hewitt.

Chapter 9. Substantial portion from *Horoscope Guide* July 1986, article "Fun With Sun And Rising Signs" by William W. Hewitt.

The author is grateful to *Horoscope Guide* and its publisher, Michelle Arnot.

TABLE OF CONTENTS

Introduction . . . . *xi*

PART I
THE BASICS

1 Astrology—The Big Picture 3
2 Natal Astrology 15
3 The Language of Astrology 23
4 Sun Sign Mini-Profiles 39
5 The Planets 61
6 The Aspects 85
7 The Houses 95

PART II
ERECTING A NATAL CHART

8 The Modern Way—By Computer 109
9 The Fast Way—By "Eyeballing" 121
10 The Original Way—By Math 135

PART III
INTERPRETING A NATAL CHART

11 Planets in the Signs 155
12 Planets in the Houses 185
13 The Aspects 213
14 Signs on the House Cusps 261
15 Putting it All Together 267
16 Transits and Progressions 271

PART IV
REFERENCE MATERIAL

17 References 275

LIST OF ILLUSTRATIONS

Figure 1—Natal Horoscope Chart 20
Figure 2—Natural Wheel 41
Figure 3—Simulated Ephemeris Page 42
Figure 4—Natal Chart with
            Intercepted Signs 110
Figure 5—Aspects & Midpoints 113
Figure 6—Patterns 114
Figure 7—Sample Computerized
            Interpretation 119
Figure 8—Eyeballing the
            Rising Sign 120
Figure 9—An Eyeballed
            Natal Chart 132
Figure 10—Simulated Table
            of Houses 138
Figure 11—Longitude Time 140
Figure 12—Table of Proportional
            Logarithms 142
Figure 13—Natal Chart 144
Figure 14—Chart Calculation 146
Figure 15—Planet Correction 150

Introduction

This book is for any one of four people:
1. The person who wants to learn enough about astrology to have fun, talk knowledgeably, and become an amateur astrology buff.
2. The person who wants to pursue astrology as a hobby.
3. The person who wants ultimately to become a professional astrologer.
4. The professional astrologer who wants to use it as a textbook for his/her beginning students.

This book is not for the person who is already well schooled in astrology unless that person wants to use it as a textbook for his/her students.

There are hundreds (perhaps thousands) of excellent books written about astrology, and if one read them all in the right sequence he/she would have an excellent education. The problem is that a person trying to learn astrology doesn't know what the right sequence is. Also, many of the books need not be read at all because they are highly specialized and technical and are of interest only to the professional who is especially interested in that narrow specialization. Many other books are reference books for just one topic such as Sun signs.

Some of the basic books are so basic that they leave one with the question, "Where do I go from here?" Other basic books quickly submerse the reader in mathematical calculations before establishing what astrology is all about in the reader's mind.

One can mentally drown in the sea of astrological information. It need not be this way. Astrology is an exciting and easy to understand science when presented in an orderly, clear, and simplified manner. The purpose of this book is to do just that.

This book does not have all the answers, but it will point you to where you can find the answers. To cover the entire subject of astrology completely would require at least 20,000 pages. I have managed to cover the basics in just a few hundred pages by leaving out vast amounts of information that a beginner does not need, and by using brief rather than wordy discussions. This book has all that 99% of you will ever need or want.

Specifically, this book:

- Tells you what astrology is and how it works.
- Teaches the basics (signs, planets, houses, aspects, etc.).
- Teaches how to interpret a natal (birth) chart.
- Briefly discusses transits, predictive astrology, and progressions.
- Shows you "eyeballing" methods for roughly determining a horoscope chart in minutes without using math.
- Has a separate chapter on how to mathematically calculate a precisely accurate horoscope chart. The method I present is simple and accurate. Essentially, you look up numbers and fill in blanks, performing simple addition and subtraction.

Most of you will not need, or want, to read this chapter because you either will not want to become professionals or you will prefer to use computerized charts.

- Discusses computerized horoscope charts. This makes astrology easy, inexpensive, and available to everyone.

- Recommends references to more detailed material for those who want to go even deeper into astrology.

The most widely practiced astrology is natal (birth) astrology. This deals with the analysis of a person's total profile as derived from certain birth information. There are many other specialized fields of astrology that deal with things like weather, catastrophes, national and international affairs, and much more.

Natal astrology is where it all starts, and this book will deal only with natal astrology. Understand this, and you can easily expand into other fields if you so choose. Probably 99% of all practiced astrology is natal astrology.

I have been practicing astrology professionally, as an avocation, since early 1974. My natal chart is used as an example in this book so you only need to study it to know all about me. The MAFA after my name signifies that I am a member of the American Federation of Astrologers.

Now turn to Chapter 1 and begin your journey into the fascinating world of the stars and you . . . the world of astrology.

William W. Hewitt, MAFA

PART I

THE BASICS

1

Astrology—
The Big Picture

This chapter gives a "big picture" of astrology today. The various astrological terms used in this chapter will, with a few exceptions, be discussed in greater detail in later chapters. The intent at this point is to give you a broad, general concept of astrology. Chapter 2 will continue with the concept, but with a narrower scope. Subsequent chapters will fill in the concept details. By the end of this book you should know the what, why, and how of astrology at a beginners level.

"What is your Sun sign?" is one of the most commonly asked questions between two people who are trying to get to know each other. Astrology fascinates people . . . they yearn to know how the heavens relate to their lives. Yet very few people have any real knowledge or understanding of astrology. To most people, astrology consists of those brief horoscope columns that appear in many newspapers and magazines. Those columns are fun, but they have little real use; they don't begin to touch on what astrology and horoscopes are all about.

Astrology is as old as measured time. There are probably as many different approaches to this fascinating subject as there are astrologers in the world today. In general, astrology embraces the idea that there is a connection between the heavens and earth—that the heavens and the earth are united, interpenetrating and sharing a common space and time. The great cosmic events happening beyond the earth (eclipses, planetary line-ups, etc.) do not cause events to occur on earth but rather reflect the events happening on earth. In other words, there is no cause in the heavens and then an effect here on earth. Planetary events are not causing events here on earth. Rather, both planetary and earthly events happen simultaneously and are mutually reflective. Neither is the cause of the other. Both are the product of the moment . . . one acted out in the heavens above, the other here on the earth below.

There is only one grand drama. The great drama enacted in the sky is also acted out, in exact detail, here on earth in the same moment. Earth is part of the cosmos and shares in that cosmic moment. All major cosmic events are interactive; that is, they represent an activity also taking place within ourself, our consciousness, and in our daily life.

Astrology is a study of heavenly cycles and cosmic events as they are reflected here in our earthly environment. The movements and cycles of the planets form a huge cosmic clock that ticks off the time and events, past, present, and future. The cosmic patterns revealed in the rhythmic motions of the planets help shed light on the seeming helter skelter of everyday life. It is easy to lose track of our direction in life due to the commotion of daily living. However, by studying our cosmic clock (astrology), we have a tool to give us better control and to see the order of things in what appears to be disorder at times.

Astrology is a study of the cycles of the Moon and

planets and the Sun and their interrelationships. There is not much in the heavens that is not cyclical—happening over and over. It is this repeating pattern that enables us to recognize heavenly events.

The Moon goes through four phases every 29 1/2 days: first quarter (New Moon); second quarter; third quarter (Full Moon); and fourth quarter. This waxing and waning of the Moon continues endlessly in an absolutely predictable pattern.

The Sun returns to the solstice points (spring, summer, autumn, and winter) predictably year after year.

Each planet has its own unique fixed orbit around the Sun that is absolutely predictable. The planets, Moon, and Sun have predictable, repeating relationships to each other in space. All of these are circles or cycles. Astrology is a study of those events where there is a return or cycling.

The cosmos is a vast clock—wheels within wheels within wheels to which we all respond. A cosmic dance that performs endlessly.

A horoscope chart is a time slice of this vast cosmic performance. The clock is stopped, in a manner of speaking. This is why the date, time, and place of birth are important. The moment of birth is a significant moment to stop the clock and examine the cosmic arrangement. Any important event is worth a cosmic snapshot. Some important dates are birth, marriage, children, etc. Any moment in time that a person considers significant is the kind of event worthy of having a horoscope chart cast for it.

By studying the planetary arrangement for a given moment, the astrologer can gain an accurate picture of what has happened on earth at that moment. This is what astrology is all about. This may sound like science fiction to you at this point, but believe me, it is very real. Astrology works! Those of you who have had a chart cast and interpreted by a competent astrologer know that it is real.

The analysis of these important moments is very complex. The mathematics needed to erect a horoscope chart is tedious and time-consuming. The best way to erect a chart is to use a computer. In later chapters I will discuss three methods of erecting a natal horoscope chart: by computer; by "eyeballing"; and the original way—hand calculated mathematics, which is how I learned.

Astrology helps us to see ourself and life in a greater perspective, to obtain the big picture. Astrology also provides very specific information to help us direct the events in our life with greater success. The remaining chapters will teach you more about this.

The more you learn about astrology, the more you will be concerned with cycles. Not only with the planetary cycles but also how these cycles show up in everyday life. The whole point of studying these cosmic cycles is to gain insight into how they appear in our lives here on earth.

All of us notice some reoccurrence or cycling effects in our lives . . . certain habits, problems and joys seem to occur to us over and over. These are the day-to-day or practical signs of the existence of cycles and our consciousness of them. Married people tend to be particularly aware of cycles since, in the ebb and flow of a very close relationship, we notice that we alternately have times of greater and less closeness. We come together and we drift apart. Again and again.

Astrology offers a new way of organizing the events in our life—a new way of seeing and understanding them. Astrology provides a way of ordering and understanding our experience. Learning to notice and take advantage of the cycles in our life can lead to an enhanced ability to handle the problems life presents. When we understand how cycles repeat themselves, how they work, we are prepared to get the most out of each phase of that cycle. Astrologers study, on the practical level, the endless ebbing and flowing . . . coming and going of these cycles in our lives. One common misconception about astrologers is that they have their heads in the clouds. It is true that we have one eye to the heavens, but, most of all, we are concerned with the here and the now, with everyday events. We have learned to notice cycles and they fascinate us. We study these cycles with great attention. Our interest in the heavens springs from our experience here on earth with the endless cycles and events surrounding us—into which each of us is born and must live.

Now I want to introduce you to some of the terms and tools of astrology. Keep in mind that the end result of astrology is to provide a tool that enables you to understand and live life better.

ASTROLOGICAL TERMS

In the introduction of this book I told you that the focus of the book is natal astrology. The primary purpose of natal astrology is to construct a horoscope chart based on specific birth data and then to interpret the meanings in the chart in order to ascertain important information about the person whose birth data was used. Thus the horoscope chart is the principal tool for natal astrology.

The horoscope chart is called by various other names also: natal chart, natal horoscope, chart wheel, radix wheel or chart, birth chart, etc. Figure 1 is a full blown natal horoscope chart. Look at it a few moments.

At this point I don't expect you to understand what you are looking at. It is probably just a confusing jumble of symbols and numbers.

We will be referring back to figure 1 many more times to explain parts of it. By the time you finish this book you will be able to read figure 1, or any other horoscope chart, with the same ease and enjoyment as when you read a novel.

For now, I just want you to know what a horoscope chart looks like. A NATAL HOROSCOPE consists of a series of mathematical calculations for the birth moment of a person. These calculations include the positions for the Sun, Moon and eight planets in the zodiac for the moment selected plus several other sensitive points (ascendant, midheaven, etc.), which will be discussed in detail later in the book. This information is arranged in a CHART WHEEL form as shown in figure 1 for the birth moment. Some of the main features of such a layout are:

CHART WHEEL: The wheel is a 360 degree picture of the heavens at the time of the birth moment. You are at the center of the wheel (the earth) surrounded by the heavens. The top of the chart or MC (MIDHEAVEN) is that part of the zodiac directly above your head while the bottom of the chart or IC (NADIR) is that part beneath your feet and on the other side of the earth from you. At the extreme left hand side of the wheel is the ASCENDANT or RISING SIGN which is that part of the zodiac that is on the horizon (rising) at the birth moment. The DECENDENT is on the right hand side of the chart; this is the part of the zodiac that is setting. The PLANETS are placed around the wheel where they appear in the zodiac in the sky at the birth moment.

In figure 1, the planets and zodiac signs are shown in symbols, known as GLYPHS in astrology. The glyphs are part of the special language of astrology, which you will learn in a later chapter. For now, just be concerned with the concepts, not the specifics.

PLANET POSITIONS: The planets are placed around the wheel in their zodiac positions. The zodiac is a convenient way to measure where a given planet is in the sky.

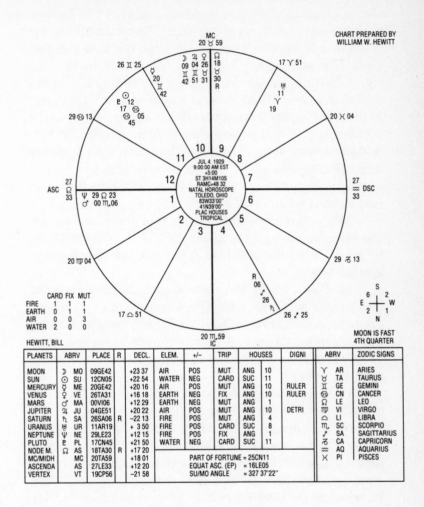

Figure 1
Natal Horoscope Chart

The zodiac stretches through all 360 degrees of the sky and is divided into the familiar l2 signs (Aries, Taurus, Gemini, etc.) of 30 degrees each. Planet positions are measured within the signs by degrees, minutes and seconds. For example, my Moon (my Moon at birth) is in the sign GEMINI (3rd sign) and in the 9th degree of Gemini and 42 minutes. My Moon is at 9 degrees and 42 minutes of the sign Gemini. You can see this in figure 1. Look at the 10th house (top of chart in the pie-slice numbered 10). You will see a symbol that looks like the moon with numbers 09♊42 below it. The "♊" represents Gemini. The 09 and 42 tell the degrees and minutes of Gemini where the moon was located when I was born.

Most chart wheels give the planet positions both on the wheel and in a list outside the wheel. As you can see in figure 1, the planet positions are also listed in a chart below the wheel.

HOUSE CUSPS: Most astrologers divide the zodiac into twleve sections or HOUSES according to a system. There are a number of HOUSE SYSTEMS used by astrologers. Proponents of one house system often feel very deeply that their method of dividing the heavens is the most significant.

To better understand the next paragraph, you need to know what a house cusp is. The word "cusp" is the name of the lines in the chart that mark the beginning of a house. The houses are those twelve pie-shaped wedges in figure 1. The natal chart is read counterclockwise starting with the ascendant (labeled ASC at the left side of figure 1), which is the horizontal line between the 12th and 1st house. Hence, the cusp of the 1st house is also the ascendant. Most systems agree that the ascendant marks the first house cusp, the descendent marks the 7th, the midheaven marks the 10th, and the nadir marks the 4th house cusp. Look at the chart wheel in figure 1 and notice how it is divided into twelve sections or Houses. The 1st house cusp is on the extreme left hand side of the wheel and the 10th house cusp is on the top. The 7th and 4th are simply opposite the 1st and 10th. The remaining house cusps (2nd, 3rd ... 5th, 6th ... 8th, 9th ... 11th, 12th) are called the intermediate house cusps because they are intermediate between the primary cusps (1st, 4th, 7th and 10th). It is these intermediate cusps that differ (in general) from one house system to another.

I'm sure all this sounds confusing, and it is. It confused me when I was a beginner. Just let it rest lightly on your mind. It will clear up as we go on. For now, I just want to give you some notion of what house cusps and house systems are. The most popular house systems in use today are the Placidian and Koch houses. The Placidian house system is used in this book. Simplistically, Placidian merely refers to a specific mathematical approach to erecting a natal horoscope chart. Give it no more concern.

AUXILIARY TECHNIQUES

The NATAL CHART captures a single moment or slice of time. There are some other techniques that can be used in conjunction with the natal chart:

TRANSITS: The natal chart can be compared to a chart that is cast for the current date. These current date charts are called TRANSIT CHARTS, and they relate the astrological factors that exist in the sky now to those that existed at the moment of your birth. Transits will be discussed only superficially in this book to give you some familiarity as a beginner. The study of transits, in my judgment, goes beyond the scope of "beginner."

PROGRESSIONS: Another popular technique is to relate the natal chart to that same natal chart as progressed into the future. As we have just seen in the preceding section, transit charts are charts progressed to a future date by the regular movement of the planets in the sky. Astrologers have a wide variety of alternate methods of progressing a chart. The "DAY FOR A YEAR" method is very popular. By this method, one day (24 hour revolution) is equated with one year (seasonal cycle) of life. Thus the 35th day after birth is considered to represent the 35th year after birth, and so on. A chart for the 35th day after birth is calculated and compared to the natal chart. This will only be discussed superficially in this book to give you some familiarity, but progressions definitely go beyond the scope of beginner.

SOLUNAR RETURNS: Another popular method is that of solar returns and lunar returns. In this technique, a chart is calculated for the precise time that the Sun (or Moon) returns to the position it had at your birth. Thus if your natal Sun was at 25 degrees and 48 minutes of the sign Cancer, a solar return chart would be one cast for when the Sun returned to this identical spot during the current year. This chart is then compared to the Natal Chart. This will not be discussed further in this book. I briefly mention it here to make you aware of the terms and because it is part of the big picture of natal astrology.

SUMMARY

This has been a very general introduction to some of the basic terms and processes used in astrology. As a beginner in astrology, a simple natal chart and interpretation is probably all you will need. In the future, you may want more complete interpretations dealing with your year ahead or perhaps a comparison report between yourself and some other person to see how compatible (or incompatible) you are. Or perhaps you will be inspired to study on your own and become more advanced or even become a professional astrologer. Elsewhere in this book I will recommend various books to help further your study if that is your desire. Those books, in turn, will lead to even more advanced study. And so it goes.

Astrology has such a broad scope and has so many facets to it, that there is something to satisfy everyone's specific desire.

But for everyone, the place to start is here—with the basics. Chapter 2 will start to bridge the gap between the "big picture" presented here in chapter 1 and the myriad of details in the chapters after 2.

Now turn the page and take your next step on the journey into yourself—into the world of natal astrology.

2

Natal Astrology

As an astrologer, I meet two kinds of people. There are those who seek me out and solicit my services to help them improve their lives in some way through astrological counseling. And then there are those who think I am an idiot for believing in astrology.

This chapter is written for both of these kinds of people. I'll briefly explain what astrology is and what it is not in simple, non-technical language. I'll discuss what astrological counseling is and how you can use this powerful tool to your advantage. There are many different types of astrology, each with its own special purpose. This chapter is confined to natal astrology, which is my specialty. Natal astrology deals with the birth patterning of individuals.

Astrology is just one of many tools we have at our disposal to help us deal with problems and enrich our lives. Some other tools are: self-hypnosis, meditation, prayer and education. Like all tools, astrology gets the job done when it is understood and used properly.

What natal astrology is:

1. A tool that provides greater understanding of self.

2. The oldest empirical science in the world.

3. A patterning of a person's innate birth potentials, strengths, weaknesses, tendencies, and probabilities. Intelligent information is available on every aspect of a person's life from cradle to grave.

What natal astrology is *not:*

1. It is *not* a cure-all.

2. It is *not* fatalistic. The individual always has the ability to choose by exercising the birthright of free will.

3. It does *not* advocate that the planets control our lives. We, through our choices, control our own lives.

The Philosophy of Astrology

I do not personally know any astrologer who thinks that planets cause events in our lives.

Astrology is based on the observation that events on earth are instantly reflected in the heavens. A simplistic analogy might be this: If you look into a mirror while trimming your eyebrows and you accidentally pierce your skin with the scissors, you will instantly see the wound bleeding in the mirror. The mirror did not cause the wound or the bleeding, did it? The mirror accurately reflected an event at the precise time the event occurred.

If it were possible to have a mirror that looked ahead in time, you could have seen the accident ahead of time and thus avoid it by exercising more care or by not trimming your eyebrows at that time.

In astrology, the heavens (the planetary positions and movements), are our mirror of earthly events. Nearly five thousand years of careful observation and record keeping have supplied us with accurate knowledge as to what kinds of earthly events are associated with what kinds of heavenly patterns.

Our astrological mirror is superior to our bathroom

mirror because the planets' patterning is constantly changing. The planets and their relationships to each other and to the earth change unendingly in an absolutely predictable way. We can mathematically calculate exactly where every planet will be at any time in relation to any point on earth. This means we have a mirror that can reflect events in the past, present, or future anywhere on earth. An awesome thought, is it not?

This powerful tool was given to us as part of creation. The planets were created as part of our world for our use. The science of astrology strives to understand and use this great gift for the benefit of humanity.

Even though it is about five-thousand years old, astrology is still in its infancy. The planet Pluto, for instance, was only discovered in February 1930, and it is still being studied. Who knows what all is out there to provide us even more information?

Still, a great deal of valuable, useful information is known and can be used to enrich our lives and help us to make better decisions and choices.

It works this way. Suppose your birth occurred at 6:44pm EST, on March 31, 1960 in Kingston, NY. The astrologer figures out mathematically where the Sun, Moon, and the eight known planets were at that moment with respect to that specific geographic point on earth. He determines that your natal Sun is at 11 degrees and 15 minutes of Aries in your sixth house; your Moon is at 5 degrees and 7 minutes of Gemini in your eighth house; and so forth for the remaining eight known planets.

The astrologer then enters the information onto a circular map known as a horoscope chart, which shows your unique horoscope patterning. Then hundreds of factors in the patterning are studied and compiled into a report known as your Natal Horoscope Analysis. This report can tell virtually everything about all aspects of your life as were reflected in the mirror of the heavens at your birth moment.

This kind of natal horoscope report can be greatly beneficial. Suppose, for example, your were unsure of what career path to pursue. Your chart will tell you in which pursuits you have the best chance of being successful, and then you can make a choice based on this knowledge rather than just shooting blindly in the dark. Predictive astrology is similar to natal astrology except that predictive astrology looks at a future date and analyzes your options at that time. This knowledge can help you avoid or lessen problems and take better advantage of opportunities.

What can astrology do to enhance a person's life? Let's examine three of the most dominant factors in the life of a person: companionship, career, and time.

The discussions on "companionship" and "career" are two actual cases of astrological counseling I performed for two clients. The discussion on "time" contains valuable information that I furnish in all my astrological counseling sessions. These will start to give you a small sampling of what astrological counseling is all about. Later in chapter 8 I have the details of my most challenging astrological assignment.

Companionship

An astrologer can do a compatibility analysis between any two people and very accurately delineate the positive and negative aspects of a given relationship. The axiom "forewarned is half armed" really applies here. The more you know about the compatibility (or incompatibility) between you and another person, the better equipped you are to interact with that person to your benefit.

I did a compatibility analysis for a young lady who was going to marry a man whom she was certain she deeply loved. Their horoscope charts showed that the mutual attraction was totally physical, very strongly so, and that they had virtually nothing else in common. In addition, his chart showed a violent temper and a sadistic nature. In spite of this, she chose to marry him. Within a few weeks after the marriage, he beat her brutally. Fortunately, she remembered my warning and left him before he could hurt her further. Astrology clearly showed her the probabilities and choices, but the choice was hers alone to make.

One can wisely use this feature of astrology to improve chances of having a harmonious and happy relationship. "Relationship" applies not only to marriage, but also to romance, friendship, business, or any sort of partnership.

But in any situation, it is the individual's choice that directs the events, not the planets. The planets show the parameters involved and the likely result of choices. But always, the individual's choice prevails. This is the least understood, and most important factor in astrology. Astrology is not fatalistic at all. The individual is in charge. The horoscope chart shows the potentials; the individual makes the choices.

Career

I have already mentioned briefly that your chart can identify your innate talents, strengths, and abilities. Often a person selects a career path because of money, family tradition, or just by chance. Rarely do these careers produce self-fulfillment. How much better it would be to select a career that takes advantage of what you have to offer and of your interests.

I did an analysis for a thirty-eight year old bachelor. He was grossly unhappy with every aspect of his life. His chart showed why. He was a mediocre, bored electronics engineer, yet his chart very strongly indicated that law enforcement was his strongest interest and latent talent. He readily admitted that he had always wanted to be a policeman since he was a young boy. But peer and parental pressure to select a career that paid well had influenced him to become an engineer. His chart showed a slight ability for engineering, hence he could do it, but it wasn't even close to being his strong suit. In addition, his chart indicated a strong materialistic streak. It also showed a love of children and a desire for marriage. He chose to let materialism dominate him; as a result he drove women away rather than attracting them. If he had his horoscope done years earlier, he would have clearly seen his probabilities and options and might have made some different choices to ensure his happiness.

Time

Many people burn up time in unproductive pursuits just to keep busy and kill excess time. Others pine away their time in loneliness. Neither situation has to be that way. Everyone is so multi-faceted in talent and interests that there is plenty of self-fulfilling activity to be engaged in. Most people do not realize this truth. They go through life as one-dimensional persons because they haven't discovered their multi-dimensional nature. A horoscope chart and analysis will clearly show each person's depth, multi-talents, abilities, etc. Armed with this knowledge, it becomes easy to select extra-curricular activities that are fulfilling and worthwhile, be it a hobby, avocation, second career, volunteer work, travel, or whatever. Again astrology presents the options—you make the choice. Some may choose to become amateur astrologers. This will eat up as much time as you choose to devote, and it is an excellent way to get to know, understand, and meet people.

There is nothing magical about this process. It is all

based on what is, on fact, on calculations, and on interpretation by a qualified person. The skill of the astrologer is the only weak link in the chain. A good astrologer will erect an accurate chart and interpret it accurately. An unskilled or careless astrologer will not do a good job. But this isn't unique to astrology, is it? The same is true of all professions. A good physician helps you get well while a poor one just drains your money or even causes problems. A competent mechanic makes your car run properly, an incompetent one doesn't.

The point is that astrology is a viable science that can be of value in your life. It merits your open-minded consideration.

Astrology does not have all the answers and is not a cure all. It is just one of many tools available for you to use in order to better orchestrate the direction of your life. It is not fatalistic. In all cases, astrology presents your options. The choice you make is always up to you alone. You alone are the Captain of your ship. Astrology merely provides a more complete map for you to set sail with.

3

The Language of Astrology

Astrology, like all scientific disciplines, has its own unique symbols, terms, and expressions. You need to gain some understanding of the astrological language now so that you will better understand the remaining chapters in this book. In chapter 1 you had some cursory exposure to a few terms. Now we are going to expand on that. After all, you want to talk and act like a professional—or at least a semi–professional—so take your time with this chapter. Let the language of astrology sink into your mind.

The Zodiac Signs

There are twelve signs of the zodiac, and each one has a glyph (symbol) and a two–letter alphabetic abbreviation as shown in the chart below. If you refer to figure 1, you will find a similar chart in the lower right corner. For practice, scan the horoscope chart and see if you can identify the zodiac glyphs using the following chart as your guide. I also include a column to show how I write the glyphs by hand.

Printed Glyph	Handwritten Glyph	Abbreviation	Zodiac Sign Name
♈	♈	AR	Aries
♉	♉	TA	Taurus
♊	♊	GE	Gemini
♋	♋	CN	Cancer
♌	♌	LE	Leo
♍	♍	VI	Virgo
♎	♎	LI	Libra
♏	♏	SC	Scorpio
♐	♐	SA	Sagittarius
♑	♑	CP	Capricorn
♒	♒	AQ	Aquarius
♓	♓	PI	Pisces

Each sign occupies 30 degrees of the horoscope wheel. Figure 2 is the natural wheel, and it shows the relationships of the signs. The cusp of the 1st house is zero degrees and zero minutes of Aries (written 00AR00). This is the beginning of the natural wheel, and it corresponds to the Spring Equinox, which is the first day of spring (approx. March 21). Spring, of course, is the natural start of the four seasons.

Reading the natural wheel counterclockwise, 30 degrees later you encounter the second house cusp at zero degrees and zero minutes of Taurus (written 00TA00). You can continue to read each cusp, in turn, counterclockwise to learn the sequential order of the zodiac signs.

The natural 4th house cusp, 00CN00, corresponds to the Summer Solstice, which is the first day of summer (approx. June 21).

The natural 7th house cusp, 00LI00, corresponds to the Fall Equinox, which is the first day of autumn (approx. September 23).

The natural 10th house cusp, 00CP00, corresponds to

the Winter Solstice, which is the first day of winter (approx. December 21).

Notice how a life cycle corresponds to the zodiac cycle. Birth – spring. Youth – summer. Adult – autumn. Senior years – winter. Remember our discussion of cycles in chapter 1. Life is a series of cycles that is mirrored in the cycles of the heavens.

The Sun moves through the zodiac at a uniform speed. Since the zodiac has only 360 degrees and a calendar year has 365 days, the Sun must progress approximately 57 minutes per day through each sign sequentially. The Sun's movement is approximately three seconds less than one degree every 24 hours. For all practical purposes (except for exact calculations) consider the Sun's movement as being one degree a day. You will see in a later chapter how this one degree per day approximation can come in handy for "eyeballing" a chart.

You can determine a person's Sun sign very quickly at a glance in figure 2. Suppose the birthdate is October 18. A glance at the natural wheel in figure 2 shows that October 18 falls between September 23 and October 23. The chart shows that the Sun sign between those dates is Libra. Thus the person's Sun sign is Libra.

If a birthdate falls on one of the dates on a house cusp in the natural wheel, you would need to erect a natal chart in order to know the person's Sun sign.

For example, a person born on June 21 might be a Gemini with the Sun at 29 degrees Gemini or a Cancer with the Sun at zero degrees Cancer because that is the day the Sun makes the transition from Gemini to Cancer. Only an accurate natal chart, using the time of day the birth occurred, will tell for sure whether the person is a Gemini or a Cancer. The same sort of thing is true for the days on all the other natural house cusps.

A person born on the day the Sun changes signs is

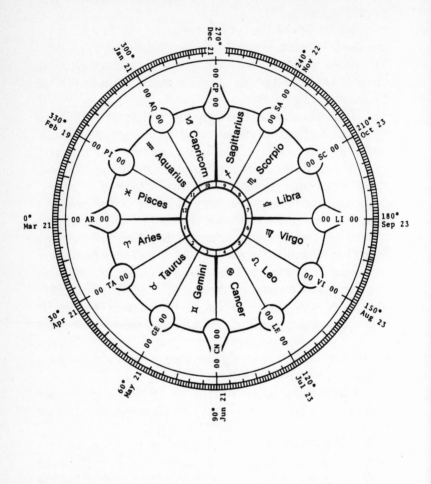

Figure 2
The Natural Wheel

said to be "born on the cusp," and that person is likely to have traits of both signs.

Degrees, Minutes, Seconds

All house cusps and all planet placements in a natal chart are made according to exactly where in a given zodiac sign they appeared at the moment of a person's birth. The placements are designated by degrees, and fractions of degrees. Minutes and seconds are fractions of degrees.

> One zodiac sign = 30 degrees
> One degree = 60 minutes
> One minute = 60 seconds

For our purposes in this book, we will not use seconds. For natal charts, most astrologers use only degrees and minutes with no significant loss of accuracy.

Look at figure 1 for this example. At the moment of my birth, my ascendant (also called rising sign) was 27♌33. This reads 27 degrees, 33 minutes of Leo. Thirty-three minutes is approximately a half degree (33 is approx. half of 60). So my ascendant is halfway between 27 degrees and 28 degrees of Leo.

The Planets

There are eight known planets currently used in astrology plus the Sun and the Moon. Technically, the Sun and Moon are luminaries, not planets. However, astrology considers the Sun and Moon to be planets for purposes of creating and analyzing natal charts. This is because the Sun and Moon act like planets in terms of their effects on the earth and its inhabitants.

So from this point on, consider that there are 10 planets. The glyphs and abbreviations for the planets are shown in the following chart. I have also included a column to show how I handwrite the glyphs.

Printed Glyph	Handwritten Glyph	Abbreviation	Planet Name
☽	☽	MO	Moon
☉	☉	SU	Sun
☿	☿	ME	Mercury
♀	♀	VE	Venus
♂	♂	MA	Mars
♃	♃	JU	Jupiter
♄	♄	SA	Saturn
♅	♅	UR	Uranus
♆	♆	NE	Neptune
♇	♇	PL	Pluto

In the above chart I have shown the modern glyph for Pluto. When you read through various other astrology books you are quite likely to encounter the original symbol for Pluto. It is ♉. Either glyph is acceptable, but most astrologers now use the newer symbol shown in the above chart. Probably the reason the Pluto symbol was changed is because the original symbol closely resembled the Mercury symbol, thereby causing confusion.

A similar chart is shown in figure 1 in the lower left corner. You are beginning to see how much valuable information is in this one computerized natal chart. A great deal more is to come throughout this book.

The Aspects

This is something we have not mentioned previously. An aspect is the relationship between two planets, expressed in degrees and minutes, at the birth moment. This relationship is very important when interpreting the meaning of a natal chart. There will be considerably more said later about aspects, but for now I just want to show you their symbols and tell you their names along with some basic facts about them.

Printed Symbol	Handwritten Symbol	Aspect Name	Degree Separation	Nature
☌	☌	Conjunction	0	Major
⚺	⚺	Semi–sextile	30	Minor
∟	∟	Semi–square	45	Minor
⚹	⚹	Sextile	60	Major
□	□	Square	90	Major
△	△	Trine	120	Major
⚼	⚼	Sesqui–square	135	Minor
⚻	⚻	Quincunx	150	Minor
☍	☍	Opposition	180	Major

In the above chart I have the name "quincunx." Another, more popular name for this same aspect is "inconjunct."

If two planets are, say, 60 degrees apart, they are said to be in sextile with each other. If the planets are 180 degrees apart, they are in opposition. And so forth. They do not have to be exactly the number of degrees apart listed in the chart. There is a plus–minus allowance; this allowance is called an orb.

The allowable orb is greatly debated among astrologers. Some astrologers say an orb of 8 degrees should be allowed for major aspects and 3 degrees for minor aspects. Others say 6 and 2, respectively. Others have individual orbs for each individual planet. A few allow 10 degrees if the Sun or Moon is involved.

In this book, and in my personal practice, I use 8 degrees for major aspects and 3 degrees for minor aspects. Of course, the closer to exact that the aspect is, the stronger is its influence in the chart. More of this later.

For example, for planets to be in sextile, they must be from 52 degrees to 68 degrees apart (8 degree orb, plus or minus). For conjunction, they must be within 8 degrees of being exactly at the same degree and sign. And so forth.

I listed all the aspects in the above chart so you would know what they are. However, in this book we will be concerned only with major aspects for the most part. I generally do not even take minor aspects into account when doing a natal interpretation unless there are so few major aspects that I must turn to the minor ones in order to get anything at all.

The aspects add an element of harmony or disharmony—ease or difficulty—smoothness or frustration—to the horoscope, depending on the aspect. This will be discussed in some detail in the chapter on aspects. For now, in general, the harmonious aspects are the trine, sextile, and semi–sextile. The difficult aspects are the square, opposition, semi–square. The conjunction can be either harmonious or not, depending on the planets involved and some other factors. More later on this.

Ephemeris

This is the single most important item you absolutely must have in order to practice astrology, even as a beginner. Without an ephemeris, you can do next to nothing of any importance.

An ephemeris is a book, or sometimes a series of books, that contains charts that show where every planet was, is, or will be for every day past, present, and future.

Figure 3 is a simulated ephemeris page that shows where every planet was on every day in July 1929. Later in this book I will show you how to read and use this page.

A typical ephemeris page gives more information than I have shown in figure 3. I deliberately did not include the additional information because I consider it beyond the scope of beginner information, and I did not want to make you any more confused than you may already be. Before you are finished with this book, we will have used all of the terms in this chapter many times over, expanding their scope of meaning and usage until you become an accomplished amateur astrologer. So don't give up. Please bear with me. I know the language of astrology can seem confusing because it is foreign and it is hard to relate to at this point. But believe me, it would be much more confusing if I were to surge ahead into chart construction and interpretation without explaining the language first.

Back to the ephemeris. You can probably check an ephemeris out of the library. Ask the librarian for assistance in finding it. Or you may wish to purchase one. I have two: One that covers the years 1900 to 1950 and one that covers the years 1950 to 2000. I'll soon be looking to purchase one that goes beyond 2000. In the beginning when I was first learning astrology in early 1974, I practically lived at the library using their ephemeris and other astrology reference books. As I became more and more experienced and started doing astrological work professionally, I purchased my own books and now have quite a nice astrology reference center in my home library. If the astrology bug bites you, you will probably do the same thing.

In this book, however, you will only need figure 3 in order to follow the examples that will be given later.

Retrograde and Direct Motion

These are terms that refer to the direction of planetary movement with relation to the earth. Direct, symbolized by the letter D, refers to the normal forward movement of planets as seen from earth. Retrograde, symbolized by the letter R, refers to the movement of planets that seem to be backing up as seen from earth. The Sun and Moon never go retrograde. All the other planets do go retrograde from time to time, and this time is very significant in doing interpretations. The planets do not actually back

JULY 1929

DAY	EPHEMERIS SIDEREAL TIME (h m s)	SU	NN	MO	ME	VE	MA	JU	SA	UR	NE	PL
1 M	18 34 14	08 CN 40	18 TA 41	18 AR 57	17 GE 31	23 TA 01	27 LE 58	04 GE 06	26 SA 20 R	11 AR 17	29 LE 18	17 CN 40
2 T	18 38 11	09 CN 37	18 TA 38	02 TA 34	18 GE 19	23 TA 59	28 LE 34	04 GE 19	26 SA 16	11 AR 17	29 LE 19	17 CN 41
3 W	18 42 07	10 CN 34	18 TA 35	16 TA 37	19 GE 11	24 TA 58	29 LE 09	04 GE 31	26 SA 12	11 AR 18	29 LE 21	17 CN 43
4 T	18 46 04	11 CN 32	18 TA 31	01 GE 05	20 GE 08	25 TA 56	29 LE 45	04 GE 44	26 SA 08	11 AR 19	29 LE 23	17 CN 45
5 F	18 50 01	12 CN 29	18 TA 28	15 GE 55	21 GE 08	26 TA 56	00 VI 21	04 GE 57	26 SA 04	11 AR 19	29 LE 24	17 CN 46
6 S	18 53 57	13 CN 26	18 TA 25	01 CN 03	22 GE 14	27 TA 55	00 VI 57	05 GE 09	25 SA 59	11 AR 20	29 LE 26	17 CN 48
7 S	18 57 54	14 CN 23	18 TA 22	16 CN 18	23 GE 37	28 TA 55	01 VI 33	05 GE 22	25 SA 55	11 AR 20	29 LE 28	17 CN 49
8 M	19 01 50	15 CN 21	18 TA 19	01 LE 30	24 GE 37	29 TA 56	02 VI 10	05 GE 34	25 SA 51	11 AR 21	29 LE 29	17 CN 51
9 T	19 05 47	16 CN 18	18 TA 15	16 LE 29	25 GE 54	00 GE 56	02 VI 46	05 GE 47	25 SA 47	11 AR 21	29 LE 31	17 CN 52
10 W	19 09 43	17 CN 15	18 TA 12	01 VI 06	27 GE 16	01 GE 56	03 VI 22	05 GE 59	25 SA 43	11 AR 22	29 LE 33	17 CN 54
11 T	19 13 40	18 CN 12	18 TA 09	15 VI 56	28 GE 42	02 GE 58	03 VI 58	06 GE 11	25 SA 39	11 AR 22	29 LE 35	17 CN 56
12 F	19 17 36	19 CN 10	18 TA 06	28 VI 56	00 CN 12	03 GE 59	04 VI 34	06 GE 23	25 SA 36	11 AR 23	29 LE 36	17 CN 57
13 S	19 21 33	20 CN 07	18 TA 03	12 LI 08	01 CN 45	05 GE 01	05 VI 11	06 GE 36	25 SA 32	11 AR 23	29 LE 38	17 CN 59
14 S	19 25 30	21 CN 04	18 TA 00	26 LI 55	03 CN 23	06 GE 03	05 VI 47	06 GE 47	25 SA 28	11 AR 23	29 LE 40	18 CN 00
15 M	19 29 26	22 CN 01	17 TA 56	07 SC 21	05 CN 03	07 GE 05	06 VI 24	06 GE 59	25 SA 24	11 AR 23	29 LE 42	18 CN 02
16 T	19 33 23	22 CN 58	17 TA 53	19 SC 31	06 CN 05	08 GE 08	07 VI 00	07 GE 11	25 SA 21	11 AR 23	29 LE 44	18 CN 04
17 W	19 37 19	23 CN 56	17 TA 50	01 SA 29	08 CN 06	09 GE 10	07 VI 37	07 GE 23	25 SA 17	11 AR 23	29 LE 45	18 CN 05
18 T	19 41 16	24 CN 53	17 TA 47	13 SA 11	10 CN 36	10 GE 14	08 VI 13	07 GE 34	25 SA 13	11 AR 23	29 LE 47	18 CN 07
19 F	19 45 12	25 CN 50	17 TA 44	25 SA 00	12 CN 08	11 GE 17	08 VI 50	07 GE 46	25 SA 10	11 AR 23 R	29 LE 49	18 CN 08
20 S	19 49 09	26 CN 47	17 TA 41	07 CP 00	14 CN 20	12 GE 20	09 VI 26	07 GE 57	25 SA 06	11 AR 23	29 LE 51	18 CN 10
21 S	19 53 05	27 CN 45	17 TA 37	18 CP 53	16 CN 16	13 GE 24	10 VI 03	08 GE 09	25 SA 03	11 AR 22	29 LE 53	18 CN 11
22 M	19 57 02	28 CN 42	17 TA 34	00 AQ 50	18 CN 16	14 GE 28	10 VI 40	08 GE 20	25 SA 00	11 AR 22	29 LE 56	18 CN 13
23 T	20 00 59	29 CN 39	17 TA 31	12 AQ 04	20 CN 19	15 GE 32	11 VI 17	08 GE 31	24 SA 56	11 AR 22	29 LE 57	18 CN 14
24 W	20 04 55	00 LE 36	17 TA 28	25 AQ 23	22 CN 23	16 GE 37	11 VI 54	08 GE 43	24 SA 53	11 AR 21	29 LE 59	18 CN 16
25 T	20 08 52	01 LE 34	17 TA 25	07 PI 23	24 CN 28	17 GE 41	12 VI 30	08 GE 54	24 SA 50	11 AR 21	00 VI 01	18 CN 17
26 F	20 12 48	02 LE 31	17 TA 21	19 PI 52	26 CN 34	18 GE 46	13 VI 07	09 GE 05	24 SA 47	11 AR 20	00 VI 03	18 CN 19
27 S	20 16 45	03 LE 28	17 TA 18	02 AR 33	28 CN 41	19 GE 51	13 VI 44	09 GE 16	24 SA 44	11 AR 20	00 VI 05	18 CN 20
28 S	20 20 41	04 LE 26	17 TA 15	15 AR 27	00 LE 48	20 GE 56	14 VI 21	09 GE 26	24 SA 41	11 AR 20	00 VI 07	18 CN 22
29 M	20 24 38	05 LE 23	17 TA 12	28 AR 39	02 LE 54	22 GE 02	14 VI 59	09 GE 37	24 SA 38	11 AR 19	00 VI 09	18 CN 23
30 T	20 28 34	06 LE 20	17 TA 09	12 TA 10	05 LE 00	23 GE 07	15 VI 36	09 GE 48	24 SA 36	11 AR 18	00 VI 11	18 CN 25
31 W	20 32 31	07 LE 18	17 TA 06	26 TA 03	07 LE 06	24 GE 13	16 VI 13	09 GE 58	24 SA 33	11 AR 18	00 VI 13	18 CN 26

Figure 3. Simulated Ephemeris Page

up, that would be impossible. But they appear from earth to back up due to their orbit in space.

In figure 3 find the Saturn and Uranus columns. Refer to your symbol chart in order to find these columns. Scan down these columns and you will see each one has an R in it.

For Saturn, the R appears at the top of the column, which indicates that Saturn was already in retrograde motion when the month of July 1929 started. Saturn continues to stay retrograde during the entire month and beyond because no D appears to indicate a change back to direct motion.

For Uranus, the R does not appear until July 18 (read across to the left to find the date). So Uranus was in direct motion until July 18 when it turned retrograde. It then stayed retrograde the remainder of the month and beyond.

Ascendant

Abbreviated ASC, the ascendant is the sign and degree of that sign that is rising on the eastern horizon at the birth moment in relation to the point on the earth where the birth takes place.

For an example, look at figure 1. In the center of the chart it tells you that I was born on July 4, 1929 at 9 am EST in Toledo, Ohio. At that moment in relation to Toledo, Ohio, 27LE33 (27 degrees and 33 minutes of Leo) was rising on the eastern horizon.

The ascendant is also called the rising sign, and it is one of the most powerful points in a natal chart. The ascendant is always the cusp of the first house and rules that house.

Midheaven

Abbreviated MC (for Medium Coeli or Meridian),

the midheaven is the highest point (directly overhead) in the zodiac at the moment of birth with relation to the point on the earth where the birth takes place.

Look again at figure 1. At 9AM on July 4, 1929 in Toledo, Ohio, 20TA59 was directly overhead and was the highest point in the zodiac.

The midheaven is also one of the most powerful points in a natal chart. The MC is always the cusp of the tenth house and rules that house.

North and South Nodes of the Moon

In figure 1 you will find a symbol that looks like this ☊ at the top of the chart near the MC. This is the symbol for the north node of the Moon. The south node is not shown in figure 1, but its symbol is an upside down version of the north node, like this ☋. The reason natal charts usually do not show the south node is because the south node is always exactly opposite the north node.

In figure 1, since the north node is shown at 18TA30R, you automatically know the south node is opposite (180 degrees away) at 18SC30R. If you look at the natural wheel in figure 2, you will see that Scorpio is exactly opposite Taurus.

Notice also that the nodes are always retrograde.

The nodes are imaginary points in space related to geomagnetic fields based on the Moon's location at the birth moment.

The nodes are used in analyzing a natal chart. Whether they are major or minor influences is debatable. I consider them to be minor.

Elements

The four elements are fire, earth, air, and water, and each of the zodiac signs falls into one of these elements.

To put this into perspective, recall that the horoscope

chart is a representation of a total life, embracing all the elements of life. Every zodiac sign appears in every horoscope, bringing the influence of that sign into the life of the person whose horoscope is represented in the horoscope chart. All signs do not carry equal weight in each horoscope, that is part of the reason each one of us is different in some way.

One of the influences that helps to make each of us a little different from others is the mix of elements in our birth charts. For example, a chart that has most of the planets in earth signs will bring a strong element of practicality to that person, while one with most planets in water signs is likely to be quite emotional or intuitive.

The following chart shows which zodiac signs belong to which element.

Fire	Earth	Air	Water
Aries	Taurus	Gemini	Cancer
Leo	Virgo	Libra	Scorpio
Sagittarius	Capricorn	Aquarius	Pisces

The Fire Signs are enthusiastic, energetic, optimistic. Fire signs are happy, lucky signs.

The Earth Signs are practical, "down to earth," realistic. Earth signs are melancholy, cautious signs.

The Air Signs are intellectual, mental, thinkers. Air signs are mentally aloof, detached signs.

The Water Signs are emotional, sensitive, feeling, intuitive. Water signs are moody, fruitful signs.

Refer now to figure 1 on page 9. In the lower left near the chart wheel there is a small chart that has the elements FIRE, EARTH, AIR, WATER listed vertically. Across from each element are numbers. Fire has 1 1 1; Earth has 0 1 1, Air has 0 0 3, Water has 2 0 0. This shows that I have three planets in fire signs, two planets in earth signs, three planets in air signs, and two planets in water signs. This is a reasonably good balance. It means my personality and behavior are not skewed strongly in one direction at the sacrifice of other characteristics. I am slightly stronger in mental pursuits (three air signs) and in drive and enthusiasm (three fire signs).

This same little chart has three columns across the top labeled CARD, FIX and MUT. We will discuss this in the very next section.

Triplicity

Each zodiac sign is associated with one of these three (triplicity) human qualities—Cardinal, Fixed, Mutable.

Cardinal people are action people. They initiate things. They move around, get things off dead center. They are not content with the status quo. They want movement, results, progress. If you wanted to hire someone to get a new project started, you would do well to hire someone with a lot of cardinal influence in their chart.

Fixed people are stable. They don't like much change. Status quo suits them fine. They will stick to things and get them done. If you want to hire someone to finish the project once it is started, you should hire someone with strong fixed influence in their chart.

Mutable people are versatile. They adapt quickly to any situation. These are the people mixers and salespersons. These people like plenty of change. They cannot stand status quo. Hire these people to be your salespersons.

Look at the same chart in figure 1 that you looked at for the elements. You can now understand what the labeling across the top of the chart means: CARD for cardinal, FIX for fixed, and MUT for mutable.

Study the chart for a few moments and you can see

that I have three planets in cardinal signs, two in fixed signs, and five in mutable signs. A fair balance. The cardinal and mutable influences are the strongest, making me enthusiastic, energetic, changeable, adaptable, etc. I am a little "down to earth" but only enough to keep my enthusiasm from getting out of hand.

You can see from this discussion of the triplicity and the elements that we are already getting into interpretation to a small degree. There will be more later on interpretation, but it is impossible to not get into it in bits and pieces while we discuss the language of astrology because language has meaning built into it.

Transits

Transits are the positions of the planets at the present moment, not as they were at birth. Transits trigger the natal chart into action or they attract minor (usually) events into our lives. To ascertain when an experience is likely to occur you compare the transit positions to the natal positions to see if there are any aspects (conjunctions, trines, sextiles, squares, oppositions, etc.) between the transits and the natal positions. We will discuss this in more detail later.

There are more astrological terms than discussed here, but I am going to stop at this point. In my judgement, we are now treading that fine line between what a beginner needs to know and what will just add confusion.

4

Sun Sign Mini-Profiles

The cornerstone of astrology interpretation is the Sun sign profile of each of the twelve zodiac signs. There are a great number of other factors that are important also such as planet placements, houses, mid-heaven, ascendant, degrees, aspects, etc. But it all starts with the Sun sign profile. Having some knowledge of all Sun signs is necessary, whether you are analyzing a chart or simply trying to understand yourself or others better.

The mini-profiles that follow are certainly not all inclusive, but they do cover salient points and provide you with a working knowledge of each sign. This will give you, the beginner, sufficient information to talk knowledgeably, analyze charts at the "big picture" level, and have a good time.

There are a number of excellent books that deal only with Sun signs in great depth, allowing 20 to 30 pages per Sun sign. In part four of this book, I recommend several of these books for your further reading if you are inclined to pursue astrology more seriously.

ARIES

Aries is the first sign of the zodiac, and the ruling plant is Mars, the planet of action. People born under the sign of Aries are action-oriented and competitive. They strive to be first in everything, often to the point of ignoring the rights and feelings of others. If they can learn to temper their aggressiveness with diplomacy and tact they can accomplish much. They are natural leaders. They like to start things for others to finish because they become bored and want to move on to some new challenge.

Aries tend to be: dynamic, impulsive, quarrelsome, easily bored, selfish, aggressive, enthusiastic, and forceful.

Some of the typical interests of Aries are: themselves, challenges of any sort, being a leader, starting things for others to finish. They have a basic pioneer nature. They also tend to be warlike.

Aries have great will power and confidence in themselves. If they can learn to love and respect others and to act with wisdom there is vitually no limit to their accomplishments.

Aries never admit defeat. They will keep on fighting and striving until they either succeed or death overtakes them. They ask no quarter, and give none.

We have had several U.S. Presidents, among them Thomas Jefferson and John Tyler, born under the sign of Aries.

Aries are the pioneers of the zodiac.

Qualities:	Cardinal-Fire
Key Phrase:	I AM!
Key Word:	Action
Virtue:	Courage
Defect:	Arrogance

Rulership: Natural ruler of the 1st house
Ruling Planet: Mars

When Aries is on any house cusp, or when any planet is in Aries, the affairs of that house or that planet will be affected by influences such as: impulsive events, energy, enthusiasm, action, perhaps even strife.

Refer to figure 1 and you can see that Aries is on my 9th house cusp and the planet Uranus is in Aries in the 8th house. So in my horoscope chart, my ninth house affairs and the action of Uranus in the 8th house are influenced to some degree by Aries. After you have read the chapters on the houses and planets and chart interpretation, this will start to make more sense. For now, just be aware that the zodiac signs influence the houses and planets involved with them.

At this point, if you just remember the Key Word, ACTION, and the ruling planet, MARS, you will have begun to understand Aries. The other salient features will quickly become part of your memory bank as you continue to work with astrology.

TAURUS

Taurus is the second sign of the zodiac and is ruled by the planet Venus, the planet of beauty and grace. Tauruses like the good things in life and usually focus their energies on acquiring material possessions and money. They pursue with great zest everything that will satisfy their desires . . . this can be pleasure, comfort, wealth.

Tauruses appreciate beautiful things whether it be art, music, nice clothing.

Tauruses are very stable people and are reliable, although usually quite stubborn.

Some of the characteristics of Taurus are: material- ism, greed, laziness, patience, practicality, steadiness and endurance. They are somewhat slow, but always finish what they start.

Some of the interests of Taurus are: comfort, posses- sions of all sorts.

These people are usually fiercely loyal to their friends, often burdening themselves with their friends' problems. They also are very jealous people, usually to the extreme.

They tend to not be too aware of themselves or their motives. They are great planners, and then they will work hard to make those plans materialize.

We have had several U.S. Presidents, among them Harry S. Truman and Ulysses S. Grant, born under the sign of Taurus.

Tauruses are the accumulators and builders
of the zodiac.

Qualities:	Fixed-Earth
Key Phrase:	I HAVE!
Key Word:	Possessions
Virtue:	Reliability
Defect:	Stubbornness
Rulership:	Natural ruler of the 2nd house
Ruling Planet:	Venus

When Taurus is on any house cusp, or when any planet is in Taurus, the affairs of that house or that planet will be affected by Taurus influences such as: profit, slow but steady progress, determination, slow to change, but dynamic when aroused, possessive attitudes.

Refer to figure 1 and you can see that Taurus is on my 10th house cusp and the planet Venus is in Taurus in that house. So in my horoscope chart, my tenth house affairs and the action of Venus are influenced to some degree by Taurus. This is an especially strong influence in my chart as you will see after you read further in the book and get into interpretations.

For now, just remember the Key Word, POSSESSIONS, and the ruling planet, VENUS, to begin understanding Taurus.

GEMINI

Gemini is the third sign of the zodiac and is ruled by the planet Mercury, the planet of mentality and communication. Geminis are probably the most intelligent people of the zodiac. They have quick minds and are curious about virtually everything. The only problem is that they rarely have any self discipline. Therefore, they lack the staying power to finish what they start. They are the "Jack of all trades, and master of none." If a Gemini acquires self discipline there is nothing he/she cannot achieve.

Geminis are the most happy when they are involved in many pursuits at the same time. Mostly they prefer intellectual activities such as philosophy, writing, talking, or thinking up things for others to do.

Geminis need to strive to acquire calmness because they are in danger of "burnout" of their nervous system since they are always stressing their nervous system so much.

Geminis tend to be: fickle, superficial, witty, inquisitive, intelligent, versatile.

Some Gemini interests are: communication of all sorts, travel, being a know-it-all, learning, talking, writing, reading.

We have had only one U.S. President, John F. Kennedy, born under the sign of Gemini.

Geminis are the salesmen and communicators of the zodiac. They are also the nonconformists of the zodiac.

Qualities:	Mutable-Air
Key Phrase:	I THINK!
Key Word:	Variety
Virtue:	Alertness
Defect:	Shallowness
Rulership:	Natural ruler of the 3rd house
Ruling Planet:	Mercury

When Gemini is on any house cusp, or when any planet is in Gemini, the affairs of that house or that planet will be affected by influences such as: much communication (writing, speaking, etc.) involved, much mental effort expended, travel, diversified interests.

Refer to figure 1 and you can see that Gemini is on my eleventh house cusp and that I have the three planets Jupiter, Moon and Mercury in Gemini in my tenth house. These are very powerful influences in my chart. With all those planets in my mid-heaven in Gemini, it is easy to see why I am a professional writer. This will become even clearer to you as you read the rest of the book.

For now, just remember the Key Word, VARIETY, and the ruling planet, MERCURY, and you will have begun to understand Gemini.

CANCER

Cancer is the fourth sign of the zodiac and is ruled by the Moon. Cancer is the most sensitive sign and is the strongest of the water signs.

Home and family life are of the utmost importance to Cancers, and they will do whatever is necessary to establish and protect their domestic security.

Cancers are easily hurt by the slights of others. These are very complex people, sometimes appearing extremely strong and at other times to be as vulnerable as a child. Very few people ever really understand Cancers; therefore they never receive the necessary understanding from others.

Cancers are very loving people. Once a love is begun, they never stop loving. However, they can be very cruel enemies. These people are usually shy, even timid, moody, and react more from intuition or emotion than from reason.

They are masters of the art of passive resistence. They can be directed through kindness, but if forced, they become immovable.

Cancers tend to be: moody, domestically and family oriented, sensitive, emotional, tenacious.

Some Cancer interests are: home, security, love of country.

We have had several U.S. Presidents, among them Calvin Coolidge and Gerald Ford, born under the sign of Cancer.

Cancers are the homemakers of the zodiac.

Qualities:	Cardinal-Water
Key Phrase:	I FEEL!
Key Word:	Tenacity
Virtue:	Caring
Defect:	Combative
Rulership:	Natural ruler of the 4th house
Ruling Planet:	Moon

When Cancer is on any house cusp, or when any planet is in Cancer, the affairs of that house or that planet will be affected by Cancer influences such as: mood changes, extreme sensitivity, "mothering" attitude, need to deal with and be recognized by the general public, often some association with food, much intuition or psychic insight.

Refer to figure 1 and you can see that Cancer is on my twelfth house cusp and that the Sun and Pluto are in Cancer in my eleventh house. We will explore how this blends in with my overall horoscope interpretation later on in the book.

For now, remember the Key Word, TENACITY, and the ruling planet, MOON, to begin to understand the Sun sign Cancer.

LEO

Leo is the fifth sign of the zodiac and is ruled by the Sun. These are noble and generous people, although they often possess oversized egos. They are over-confident, blunt, and outspoken. These characteristics often cause them to lose friends. Leos are courageous and loyal. They like to be in charge.

Leos are strongly attracted to the opposite sex.

Woe be unto anyone who hurts a Leo's child!

Leos tend to be: romantic, idealistic, ambitious, egotistical, tempermental, loyal, enthusiastic, generous, optimistic, domineering, affectionate.

Some Leo interests are: sports and games, achievement, fun, being in the spotlight, children (especially theirs).

We have had several U.S. Presidents, among them Herbert Hoover and Benjamin Harrison, born under the sign of Leo.

Leos are the entertainers (sometimes clowns) of the zodiac. They are also the "ones in charge."

Qualities:	Fixed-Fire
Key Phrase:	I WILL!
Key Word:	Power
Virtue:	Magnanimous or Noble
Defect:	Ostentatious or show-offs
Rulership:	Natural ruler of the 5th house
Ruling Planet:	Sun

When Leo is on any house cusp, or when any planet is in Leo, the affairs of that house or planet will be affected by Leo influences such as: enjoyment, kinglike rulership, romance, flamboyancy, pomp, optimism, faith, tempermental reactions, events concerning children.

Refer to figure 1 and you can see that Leo rules my ascendant (first house) and that the planet Neptune is in Leo in the first house. This is a powerful influence in my life as you shall discover later on in the book.

For now, remember the Key Word, POWER, and the ruling planet, SUN, to begin to understand the Sun sign LEO.

VIRGO

Virgo is the sixth sign of the zodiac and is ruled by the planet Mercury. Virgos constantly search for knowledge.

Virgos are very detail conscious and do well in any line of work that requires exactness. Virgos are practical and efficient.

The single greatest defect of Virgo is that they are very critical of others . . . even judgemental of others. If they overcome this negative trait they can attain the highest of spiritual achievement in life.

Sometimes they become so immersed in detail that they lose sight of the big picture. They also tend to worry a lot which can adversely affect their health. If they learn to discipline their minds to think constructive thoughts, they then usually have very good health and be of great benefit to humanity. Virgos often go into some branch of the medical profession.

Probably more Virgos remain unmarried than any of the other signs because they have difficulty in finding anyone who measures up to their high standards.

Virgos tend to be: critical, methodical, neat, reliable, practical, mental, industrious, and cautious.

Some Virgo interests are: fault finding, helping to improve others, work, details, perfection.

We have had several U.S. Presidents born under the sign of Virgo, among them William H. Taft and Lyndon B. Johnson.

Virgos are the craftsman of the zodiac.

Qualities:	Mutable-Earth
Key Phrase:	I ANALYZE!
Key Word:	Service
Virtue:	Thoroughness
Defect:	Pettiness or Fussiness
Rulership:	Natural ruler of the 6th house
Ruling Planet:	Mercury

When Virgo is on any house cusp, or when any planet is in Virgo, the affairs of that house or that planet will be affected by Virgo influences such as: much discrimination, caution, analysis, work, seeking perfection, health, efficiency, details, craftsmanship, seeking flaws.

Refer to figure 1 and you can see that Virgo is on the cusp of my 2nd house and that the planet Mars is in Virgo in my 1st house. This is a strong influence in my chart, and you will see how as you progress through the book.

Remember for now that the Key Word is SERVICE and the ruling planet is MERCURY.

LIBRA

Libra is the seventh sign of the zodiac and is ruled by the planet Venus, the planet of beauty and grace.

Libras are rarely loners; they want and need companionship. Thus marriage is very important to them. Also, they prefer an occupation that brings them in partnership with others or at least brings them in close contact with others. They make good counselors and judges because they can clearly see both sides of an issue. However, this ability to see an issue from all sides frequently gives them a problem in making decisions, especially concerning minor matters. For instance, it may take a Libra hours just to pick out a blouse or shirt when there is a selection to choose from.

Libras are rarely lazy. They work hard, and also demand that their partners work just as hard. They have a strong sense of justice and fair play. They rarely express anger, but when they do it is usually a "storm." Their anger subsides quickly, however, and they do not hold grudges. Anger frequently leaves them feeling ill.

Libras tend to be: romantic, dependent, fickle, cooperative, gracious, extravagant, somewhat materialistic.

Some of the Libra interests are: partnerships, justice, peace, companionship, beauty, social life.

We have had several U.S. Presidents, among them Dwight D. Eisenhower and James E. Carter, born under the sign of Libra.

Libras are the diplomats of the zodiac.

Qualities:	Cardinal-Air
Key Phrase:	I BALANCE!
Key Word:	Harmony
Virtue:	Fairness
Defect:	Indecisiveness
Rulership:	Natural ruler of the 7th house
Ruling Planet:	Venus

There are two correct ways to pronounce Libra: lee-bra or lie-bra. The "lee-bra" pronunciation is the one most often used by most people. However, the "lie-bra" pronunciation is the one most often used by professional astrologers and well informed amateur astrologers. So if you want to sound like a well informed astrologer, say "lie-bra."

When Libra is on any house cusp, or when any planet is in Libra, the affairs of that house or that planet will be affected by Libra influences such as: partnerships, joint enterprises, refined harmony, balance, fairness, beauty, sometimes idealistic or romantic to the extreme.

Refer to figure 1 and you can see that Libra is on the cusp of my third house. I have no planets in Libra. The influence of Libra in my chart is subtle and hardly even noticed. I'll point out the influence in the chapter on interpreting the natal chart.

To start understanding Libra, remember the Key Word, HARMONY, and the ruling planet, VENUS.

SCORPIO

Scorpio is the eighth sign of the zodiac and is ruled by the planet Pluto. This is an extremely strong sign; no sign is so potent for good or for evil as is Scorpio.

Scorpios have strong will power and an intense emotional drive. Their sex drive and their interest is sex is usually very strong. Scorpios are not "half-way" people; whatever they do, they do it with intensity and completeness. They have no fear of death.

Because of their strong emotional drive, they need to keep their integrity high else they fall into undesireable behavior such as violence, jealousy, hatred, or possessiveness.

These people often become workaholics. They drive themselves hard, and usually drive others unmercifully. They despise weakness in self or others.

Often they will help others, but then they expect the one who was helped to start helping themselves. They will give a helping hand, but not for long.

Scorpios are secretive people. They also are ruthless enemies or competitors.

Scorpios tend to be: vindictive, sarcastic, heroic, forceful, cynical, secretive, determined, suspicious.

Some Scorpio interests are: sex, unraveling mysteries, money of others, being the unseen power.

There have been more U.S. Presidents born under the sign Scorpio than under any other sign. Two of these were Theodore Roosevelt and John Adams.

Scorpios are the detectives of the zodiac.

Qualities:	Fixed-Water
Key Phrase:	I DESIRE!
Key Word:	Resourcefulness
Virtue:	Intense dedication
Defect:	Vindictiveness
Rulership:	Natural ruler of the 8th house
Ruling Planet:	Pluto

When Scorpio is on any house cusp, or when any planet is in Scorpio, the affairs of that house or that planet will be affected by Scorpio influences such as: secrecy, coercion, deep emotion and desires, jealousy, fighting to the death, possessiveness, forced changes, sometimes a fatalistic attitude, sometimes an area where meanness prevails.

Refer to figure 1 and you can see that Scorpio is on the cusp of my 4th house. I do not have any planets in Scorpio. The subtle influence of Scorpio in my horoscope chart will be better understood when you get to the chapter on interpretation.

Remember the Key Word is RESOURCEFULNESS and the ruling planet is PLUTO.

SAGITTARIUS

Sagittarius is the ninth sign of the zodiac and is ruled by the planet Jupiter, the planet of expansiveness and good fortune.

Sagittarians are honest and freedom loving. No matter how difficult a situation becomes, there always seems to be help for the Sagittarian because they seem to always be under some sort of protective shield.

These are generally spiritual people, but they sometimes become narrow minded if they are associated with a social or religious group that has limited vision.

These people call the shots as they see them without any embellishment; therefore, they are often considered to be blunt or lacking in tact.

Women Sagittarians make charming companions, but usually dislike domestic tasks and are generally quite independent.

These are idealistic people. They must learn wisdom and balance or else they can become fanatics and follow blindly some narrow dogma.

Peple born under the sign of Sagittarius tend to be: optimistic, friendly, argumentative, generally easy-going.

Some Sagittarius interests are: religion, philosophy, traveling (especially foreign), horses, law, books, publishing, giving advice.

We have had several U.S. Presidents, among them Zachary Taylor and Martin VanBuren, born under the sign of Sagittarius.

Sagittarians are the philosophers of the zodiac.

Qualities:	Mutable-Fire
Key Phrase:	I SEE!
Key Word:	Freedom
Virtue:	Hopefulness
Defect:	Non-discriminating
Rulership:	Natural ruler of the 9th house
Ruling Planet:	Jupiter

When Sagittarius is on any house cusp, or when any planet is in Sagittarius, the affairs of that house or that planet will be affected by Saggittarian influences such as: good fortune, abundance, optimism, lack of discrimination, where hunches play a significant role, foreign people or things, helping others to find themselves, philosophy, humor.

Refer to figure 1 and you can see that Sagittarius is on my 5th house cusp and that the planet Saturn is in Sagittarius in my 4th house. This plays a significant role in my horoscope chart as you will see later.

Remember that the Key Word is FREEDOM and the ruling planet is JUPITER.

CAPRICORN

Capricorn is the tenth sign of the zodiac and is ruled by the planet Saturn. Many astrologers consider this to be the strongest sign of the zodiac. These people are frugal, hard working, and dedicated to achieving their goals. If they maintain integrity, they can achieve the highest of accomplishments. If they lack integrity, they may also achieve the highest accomplishments, but they will assuredly have the greatest of falls. A recent example of this is Richard Nixon, a Capricorn, who became president and was forced from office because of his lack of integrity. This is because the ruling planet, Saturn, always gives perfect justice . . . what you sow, you will reap. Sow good seed, and you reap good results. Sow bad seed, and you reap undesireable results.

These are practical people. They will let nothing stand in their way. They are undefeatable enemies and loyal friends. They are neat and methodical. They also are frequently "slave drivers."

They do not function well for long in subordinate positions. They need to be in charge, even if it is in a small way. Capricorns, as a rule, live to a ripe old age. They are old when they are young, and young when they are old.

Capricorns tend to be: serious, frugal, ambitious, realistic, cautious, responsible, worriers, hard working.

Some Capricorn interests are: business, material success, being in charge.

We have had several U.S. Presidents, among them Andrew Johnson and Woodrow Wilson, born under the sign of Capricorn.

Capricorns are the organizers of the zodiac.
Qualities: Cardinal-Earth
Key Phrase: I USE!

Key Word: Ambition
Virtue: Respectfulness
Defect: Condescending
Rulership: Natural ruler of the 10th house
Ruling Planet: Saturn

When Capricorn is on any house cusp, or when any planet is in Capricorn, the affairs of that house or that planet will be affected by Capricornian influences such as: self-discipline, ambition, coldness, serious attitude, desire for status, frugality, in some cases cheapness, public ambitions, hard work, responsibility.

Refer to figure 1 and you can see that Capricorn is on the cusp of my fifth house. I have no planets in Capricorn. This is a subtle influence in my chart.

Remember the Key Word is AMBITION and the ruling planet is SATURN.

AQUARIUS

Aquarius is the eleventh sign of the zodiac and is ruled by the planet Uranus. This is the sign of brotherhood and friendship. They are loyal friends.

These are tireless workers, and prefer to work in some endeavor that has humanitarian benefits. They have great desire for material gain, but are not greedy. They are willing to work for what they want, and do not demand more than their fair share. Because they take their work seriously, they are usually a bundle of nerves inside; this can make them get ill frequently. However, to outward appearances, they seem to be calm.

With Aquarians, what you see is what you get . . . they do not put on facades or affectations. They have great dislike for hypocricy.

These are determined, stubborn, and often argumentative people. They have the ability to stir up much dislike toward themselves.

People born under the sign of Aquarius tend to be: tactless, independent, naive, broadminded, dogmatic, rebellious, impersonal.

Some Aquarian interests are: helping others, friends, astrology, truth, politics.

We have had several U.S. Presidents, among them Abraham Lincoln and Franklin D. Roosevelt, born under the sign of Aquarius.

Aquarians are the reformers of the zodiac.

Qualities:	Fixed-Air
Key Phrase:	I KNOW!
Key Word:	Independence
Virtue:	Friendliness
Defect:	Eccentricity
Rulership:	Natural ruler of the 11th house
Ruling Planet:	Uranus

When Aquarius is on any house cusp, or when any planet is in Aquarius, the affairs of that house or that planet will be affected by Aquarian influences such as: need for freedom and independence, unconventional behavior or attitudes, humanitarian ideals, artistic talents displayed, friends, sudden changes and events, expensive tastes, much originality and inventiveness, use of scientific and electrical methods.

Refer to figure 1 and you can see that Aquarius is on my 7th house cusp and that I have no planets in Aquarius. This influence is very minor in my chart.

Remember the Key Word is INDEPENDENCE and the ruling planet is URANUS.

PISCES

Pisces is the twelfth sign of the zodiac and is ruled by the planet Neptune. These are very sensitive people who are responsive to the thoughts and feelings of others. They always want to do the right things, but usually have little will power. They are unable to make up their own minds.

These people rarely participate in sports or strenuous activity. They are not combative. They will suffer rather than fight for their rights; they have a martyr complex.

They can be so stubborn that no one can reason with them. They also like to drift, rather than buckle down to a responsibility.

They alternate between pessimism and optimism. In fact, they alternate in much of their behavior from one extreme to the other; this is very annoying to anyone who has to live or work with them.

Generally, these are not ambitious people; they seem to be tuned in to some dream world. They often make excellent artists in all fields of art. They have overactive imaginations.

Pisces are blind to any faults in anyone they love.

Pisces tend to be: sensitive, impressionable, changeable, day-dreaming, compassionate, psychic, careless, dependent.

Some interests of Pisces are: hospitals, medicine, pets, drugs, just thinking, serving others.

We have had several U.S. Presidents, among them George Washington and Andrew Jackson, born under the sign of Pisces.

Pisceans are the martyrs of the zodiac.

Qualities:	Mutable-Water
Key Phrase:	I BELIEVE
Key Word:	Compassion
Virtue:	Charitableness
Defect:	Easily influenced
Rulership:	Natural ruler of the 12th house
Ruling Planet:	Neptune

When Pisces is on any house cusp, or when any planet is in Pisces, the affairs of that house or that planet will be affected by influences such as: subject to sympathy and understanding, mystical experiences, activities behind the scenes, fraud, idealism at the expense of practicality, activity concerned with drugs, sick people, institutions, secrets or secret activities.

Refer to figure 1 and you can see that Pisces is on the cusp of my 8th house. I do not have any planets in Pisces. The Piscean influence in my chart is subtle.

Remember the Key Word, COMPASSION, and the ruling planet, NEPTUNE.

RULERSHIP OF THE PHYSICAL BODY PARTS

Medical astrology is a special field of astrology that requires considerable knowledge and ability that is far beyond the beginner stage. However, the beginner should be aware that the various body parts are ruled by the zodiac signs.

It may also be helpful to know some of those key rulerships. The following listing delineates the parts of the body ruled by each sign. This is just for your reference and to make you aware. Medical astrology will not be discussed further in this book.

> *Aries:* head, face (except nose), brain
> *Taurus:* neck, throat, thyroid gland
> *Gemini:* shoulders, arms, hands, lungs, thymus
>   gland, bronchial tubes
> *Cancer:* stomach, breasts
> *Leo:* heart, spine
> *Virgo:* intestines, bowels
> *Libra:* kidneys, ovaries
> *Scorpio:* nose, bladder, sex organs, adenoids

Sagittarius: hips, thighs, muscles, sciatic nerves
Capricorn: skeletal structure, skin
Aquarius: legs and ankles, blood circulation, electricity of the body, eye retina
Pisces: feet, toes, lymph glands, sweat glands

The preceding list is just the tip of the iceberg of a very specialized field in astrology, but it should give you some appreciation of the vast scope of astrology.

5

The Planets

Each of the planets has its own unique basic characteristics that it carries with it regardless of which house or in which sign it appears.

Of course, the action of each planet varies because its influence blends with, and is influenced by, the action of its respective sign and house. The aspects a planet makes with other planets are also a "modifiying influence."

However, the basic characteristics of each planet will be strong enough to be apparent in every horoscope chart, regardless of these influences.

In this chapter we will explore the salient characteristics of each planet. The better you understand the nature of the planets (and the signs, aspects, and houses) the better you will be at reading and interpreting horoscope charts.

All of the characteristics of a given planet will not apply to every chart. Only those characteristics unique to the person involved will apply. The placement of the planet in the chart by house and sign, and the aspects it makes to other planets determine exactly which characteristics will apply.

The descriptions in this chapter touch only on some of the key characteristics. You will need to read books devoted more completely to planets in order to gain more complete knowledge. However, at the beginner stage, this chapter has sufficient information to allow you to begin to interpret charts and have a reasonably good amateur knowledge of astrology.

SUN

The Sun is the single most important planet in the natal chart because it represents your ego and individuality. It represents, by its house and sign placement, where you have the ability to "shine." It shows your ambitions and deepest character traits. It represents your vitality.

A strong Sun in a chart can overcome much weakness or adversity elsewhere in the chart.

A weak Sun in a chart makes it more difficult for a person to achieve goals.

Let me digress briefly to discuss a weak Sun. What I say here also applies to any planet that may be weakly placed in the horoscope.

One example of a weakly placed Sun would be: Sun in Libra and placed in whatever house in the chart is ruled by Aquarius, and where there are no major aspects to the Sun from any other planet.

Without regard to the rest of the horoscope chart, a person with this Sun would not have much will power, would probably not have much charm.

However, there are nine other planets in the horoscope, and they can help to overcome a weak Sun.

For example, Mars conjunct Venus in the 1st house could do wonders for providing some charm. A well placed Pluto could provide some will power. And so forth. There are a great many combinations of planet aspects and placements that could help compensate for this weak Sun.

The point is that in any given chart there may be a planet or two that is weak. The remaining planets more often than not are able to compensate for some weakness. And in all cases: NO PLANET IS COMPLETELY POWER-LESS IN A CHART, REGARDLESS OF ITS PLACEMENT. A planet may have less power in some charts, but it is never without some power.

You have probably noticed some people who seem to have little or no difficulty at all in achieving goals. Others seem to have great difficulty. Often the difference is that the Sun (or other planets) in one chart are more strongly placed than in the other chart.

In general, the Sun functions more powerfully in Leo, Aries, and Sagittarius.

In general, the Sun functions with more difficulty in Aquarius, Libra, and Gemini.

In the other six signs (Taurus, Cancer, Virgo, Scorpio, Capricorn, and Pisces), it seems to hit a happy medium between easy and difficult.

Some Solar characteristics are: ambition, confidence, strength, leadership, desire for recognition, individuality.

Some positive characteristics of the Sun are: dignity, generousity, will power, loyalty, fairness, honor.

Some negative characteristics of the Sun are: jealousy, conceitedness, arrogance, laziness, obstenence.

The Sun rules Leo. It also rules the heart, spine, sperm, and genetic inheritance.

The Sun moves through all twelve zodiac signs each year, progressing approximately one degree a day (53 seconds a day is more exact). It spends approximately 30 days in each zodiac sign. The Sun never goes retrograde.

If you look at figure 1 you will see that my Sun is placed in the 11th house in Cancer. This, among other

things, says that my ability to "shine" will be in relation to
11th house and Cancer matters. The 11th house is a public
house, and it has to do with dealing with the public at
large and groups of people. (You will learn more about the
11th house in a later chapter.) Cancer, among other things,
has to do with the home and with psychic matters.

Now let's examine what I do for a living. I write
books in my home, books that go out to the world at large.
Three of my published books to date deal with psychic
matters. I also lecture to groups of people on these subjects.

Are you beginning to see what kinds of information
can be gleaned from a natal chart?

Are you beginning to see how to start interpreting
planets in signs and houses?

With the discussion of each planet, I will delve into
this sort of interpretation a little so you start to get the feel
of astrology. Then later on we will go deeper into interpretation.

MOON

Next to the Sun, the Moon is the most personal of
the planets and has great effect on a person. It shows the
everyday activities of life—how you get along with people, especially with women (regardless of your gender).
The Moon shows where your strong emotional attach-
ments are. In a man's chart, the Moon (and Venus) placement shows the type of woman he is drawn to. In a woman's chart, the Moon (and Mars) for the type of man she is
drawn to.

Where the Moon is placed by sign and house indicates where there is a strong, major interest in life. The
Moon's position in a natal chart also shows what area of
life will have many fluctuations and changes, and where
there will be a strong drive to achieve stability and security.

The Moon's position in the chart also indicates how the public will react to the person.

The Moon affects moods, memory, and subconscious thoughts. The Moon represents the mother, domestic matters, and home life.

In general, the Moon functions more powerfully in Cancer, Taurus, and Pisces.

In general, the Moon functions with more difficulty in Capricorn, Scorpio, and Virgo.

In the other six signs (Aries, Gemini, Leo, Libra, Sagittarius, and Aquarius), it seems to hit a happy medium between easy and difficult.

Basic Lunar types are: emotional, sensitive, imagination, domestic, instictive, and changeable.

Some positive characteristics of the Moon are: inspiration, magnetism, visionary and positive psychic powers, flexibility, amourousness, creativity.

Some negative characteristics of the Moon are: self-destructive or negative psychic powers, dreaminess, moodiness, possessiveness, smothering love, tendency to be clannish.

The Moon rules Cancer. It also rules nutrition, stomach, breasts, womb and impregnation, body fluids, subconscious mind, insanity, instincts, memory, and digestion.

The Moon moves through all twelve zodiac signs about every 28 days, progressing about 12 to 15 degrees a day (the speed varies). It spends about 2 1/2 days in each zodiac sign, and it never goes retrograde.

Refer to figure 1. My Moon is in Gemini in the 10th house. The Moon shows, among other things, where a person's major interest in life is and what occurs in a person's daily activities.

Gemini rules communications (talking, writing, etc.) among other things. One of the 10th house matters is what we do in life that is exposed to public view. (More about the 10th house in a later chapter.)

My daily activity is writing, and writing is my major interest. The public views me as an author. It all fits, doesn't it?

In addition, I receive letters from my readers from all over the United States and from many other countries. And 99% of my letters are from women. That fits, too, doesn't it?

Astrology really works!

MERCURY

Like the Sun and the Moon, Mercury is a personal planet. Mercury rules the conscious, reasoning mind. Mercury's house and sign placements show how the mind directs its thoughts. Mercury reflects our link of reason between the conscious and subconscious, between physical and spiritual.

As we think, so we become. Mercury in the chart depicts our thinking process.

Mercury's links (aspects) with other planets give further description of our thought processes. For example, a strong link with Saturn shows a serious thinker.

If Mercury is in close aspect with another planet, it becomes strongly influenced by that planet and becomes a channel through which the other planet expresses its power. When powerfully placed by sign, house position, or aspect, Mercury becomes an extremely powerful influence in the chart.

People who are slow witted or who have great difficulty in learning or understanding often have a poorly placed Mercury in their chart. If Mercury is in a strong adverse aspect with other planets, it is very difficult for the person to use their mental faculties to their best advantage.

In general, Mercury functions most powerfully in Gemini, Virgo, Aquarius, and Scorpio.

In general, Mercury functions with more difficulty in Sagittarius, Pisces, Leo, and Taurus.

In the other four signs (Aries, Cancer, Libra, and Capricorn), it seems to hit a happy medium between easy and difficult.

Mercurial types tend to be: adaptable, mental, active, able pursue several activities simultaneously, expressive, communicative.

Some positive characteristics of Mercury are: ability to learn quickly, resourcefulness, brilliance, eloquence, dexterity, and great awareness.

Some negative characteristics of Mercury are: an unwarranted sense of superiority, indecisiveness, instability, talks too much, gullable, and nosy.

Mercury rules both Gemini and Virgo. It also rules the nervous system, tongue movement, hands, reflexes and coordination, mental awareness, memory, and the conscious mind.

Mercury goes through all twelve zodiac signs in approximately one year, never getting further away from the Sun than 28 degrees. Mercury goes retrograde for approximately three weeks each time, about four times a year. Because of this, Mercury sometimes is ahead of the Sun and sometimes trails the Sun. Mercury is sometimes the "morning star" and sometimes the "evening star."

Mercury travels from 0 degrees to 2 degrees 12 minutes a day, depending on whether it is retrograde or in fast direct motion. This means Mercury stays in one zodiac sign from 14 to a little over 30 days, again depending on the motion.

In figure 1 you can see that my Mercury is in Gemini in the 10th house. This is an especially powerful placement because Mercury is in the sign it rules (Gemini) and is in the powerful midheaven (10th house).

Mercury rules writing (among other things) and is in the public 10th house. And what do I do for a living? Right—I am a writer who writes books for the public.

Once again, you can see how astrology can accurately detail a person's life.

VENUS

Venus is also a personal planet. It typically shows where money may be gained or spent.

Venus represents refinement, harmony, love, beauty, and artistry. It shows how you will interact with other people.

In a man's chart, Venus, along with the Moon, shows the kind of women he will be attracted to and possibly marry. See Mars to find the kind of man a woman is attracted to.

Venus is often called the lesser benefactor. This means it is associated with good fortune in minor ways. For example, winning a small amount of money in the lottery. Its house position shows where good luck can appear.

In general, Venus functions most powerfully in Taurus, Libra, Pisces, and Aquarius.

In general, Venus functions with more difficulty in Aries, Scorpio, Virgo, and Leo.

In the other four signs (Gemini, Cancer, Sagittarius, and Capricorn), it seems to hit a happy medium between easy and difficult.

Venus rules over: romance, love, gentleness, beauty, sociability.

Some positive characteristics of Venus are: charm, refinement, consideration, creativity, inspiration, graceful movement.

Some negative Venus characteristics are: vanity, laziness, jealousy, self-indulgence, indecisiveness, possessiveness.

Venus rules both Taurus and Libra. It also rules ovaries, throat, and blood circulation.

Venus moves through all twelve zodiac signs in approximately one year, never getting further away from the Sun than 48 degrees. Like Mercury, Venus goes retrograde and sometimes is ahead of the Sun and sometimes trails the Sun. Venus, too, may be the "morning star" sometimes and she "evening star" at other times.

Venus travels from 0 degrees to 1 degree 16 minutes a day, depending on whether it is retrograde or not. This means Venus stays in one zodiac sign from 23 days to a little over two months, depending on its motion.

You can see in figure 1 that my Venus is in Taurus in the 10th house. This is a powerful placement. Among other things, this indicates that I will earn my money by doing something creative (writing in my case) for the public.

In a man's chart, I mentioned that Venus and the Moon indicate the kind of woman he is likely to marry. My Venus is in Taurus, and I am married to a woman who has a Taurus ascendant in her natal chart. Further, my Moon is in Gemini (talkative people), and my wife is very talkative. I like talkative women. At this writing, we have been happily married for 40 years. I guess it pays to flow with the energies expressed in the natal chart, does it not?

By now you can see the pattern forming. Each planet placement is reinforcing other planet placements in my chart. Even without looking further, you can easily conclude that I will be a successful professional author.

MARS

Mars is action, energy and courage. It represents our most primative and aggressive urges. It also strongly influences sexual matters.

The Mars placement in a natal chart shows where physical activity will take place and indicates the kind of things that will arouse you—how you react to violence, etc.

In a woman's chart, Mars describes the kind of man she will be most physically attracted to. It also describes how she will get along with such a man—harmoniously or not. See the Moon and Venus for the kind of woman a man is attracted to.

Any aspect between Mars and the Sun in a chart gives strong will power and a strong physical constitution.

Mars in aspect to any planet gives a great deal of energy to the action of the other planet—this may be good or not so good, depending on the specific chart.

In general, Mars functions more powerfully in Aries, Capricorn, and Leo.

In general, Mars functions with more difficulty in Libra, Cancer, and Aquarius.

In the other six signs (Taurus, Gemini, Virgo, Scorpio, Sagittarius, and Pisces), it seems to hit a happy medium between easy and difficult.

Mars types tend to be: forceful, independent, strong, desiring, courageous, impulsive, energetic.

Some positive characteristics of Mars are: determination, self-reliance, an aggressive nature, bold, and devoted.

Some negative characteristics of Mars are: jealousy, stubbornness, violence, destructive, warlike, cruel.

Mars rules Aries. It also rules surgery, red blood cells,

tolerance for pain, muscular energy, certain diseases that cause pain, fevers and inflammations.

Mars moves through all twelve zodiac signs in approximately two years, staying in one sign an average of 1.5 months.

Mars travels from 0 degrees to 1 degree 16 minutes a day, depending on whether it is in retrograde or direct motion.

Figure 1 shows that my Mars is in Virgo in the 1st house. This is a powerful placement because it is in the first house which Mars rules normally (see the Natural Wheel in figure 2) and Mars is in close conjuction with my ascendant and with Neptune. We will discuss the specifics of this later in the chapter on chart interpretations.

Mars in Virgo is a common placement in the charts of surgeons and various craftsmen such as carpenters, engravers, etc. From this, you might hastely conclude that I am skilled with my hands in some way. Nothing could be further from the truth—I am usually quite clumsy and inept in using my hands.

 Mars in Virgo does confer skill and craftsmanship, but in my case it is craftsmanship with words, not with things.

I point this out to impress the point that when you interpret a natal chart you should not be too quick to make the obvious interpretation. You must study the entire chart carefully and look for subtilties.

In my chart there is not one other indication that I might be skilled with my hands, but there is plenty of other evidence that I am skilled with words. Thus you can conclude that Mars in Virgo in my chart gives power and energy to my ability with crafting words.

JUPITER

Jupiter is planet of expansiveness. Wherever it is placed in a natal chart, it shows where there will be an abundance in the person's life. It could be an abundance of wealth, or poverty. Good health or poor. Success or failure, etc. In other words, wherever Jupiter's influence is, there will be a great deal of whatever factors Jupiter is affiliated with in that specific natal chart.

Jupiter is sometimes called the greater benefactor because it is associated with good fortune in major ways. For this reason, Jupiter is more often a benefit in a chart than it is a detriment.

Jupiter's placement in a chart shows where the greatest luck can be found. It also shows where the person is least likely to be cautious or discriminating.

Jupiter is associated with religion and philosophy. It also rules legal matters, foreign affairs, long distance and foreign travel, horses, books, printing and publishing.

Jupiter in aspect to any planet gives a great deal of good fortune and expansiveness to the action of the other planet in the person's chart.

In general, Jupiter functions more powerfully in Sagittarius, Cancer, Taurus, and Pisces.

In general, Jupiter functions with more difficulty in Gemini, Capricorn, Virgo, and Scorpio.

In the other four signs (Aries, Leo, Libra, and Aquarius), it seems to hit a happy medium between easy and difficult.

Some basic Jupiter characteristics are: optimism, good fortune, confidence; a generous nature, honorable, and aspiring.

Some positive characteristics of Jupiter are: success, ambition, dignity, wealth, inspiration, reverence.

Some negative Jupiter characteristics are: extravagance, pomposity; tendency to be fanatical, conceited, very lazy, and overconfident.

Jupiter rules Sagittarius. It also rules fat, growths, pancreas, liver, hips, and thighs, and insulin.

Jupiter moves through all twelve zodiac signs in approximately 12 years, staying in one sign an average of one year.

Jupiter travels from 0 degrees to 14 minutes a day, depending on whether it is in retrograde or direct motion.

Figure 1 shows that my Jupiter is in Gemini in the 10th house. Recall that Jupiter functions with difficulty when in Gemini. Let's see what this means in my chart.

First, Jupiter rules books and publishing. Gemini rules communication (writing). So you can quickly and accurately conclude that I am going to be an author of books that do get published.

However, the Jupiter/Gemini combination says "with difficulty." And indeed this has been true. I have had great difficulty in becoming successful as a writer. My first book was not published until I was 57 years old.

However, there is a bright side to this. Jupiter in the 10th house also indicates success in the latter part of one's life, which is where I am. So the difficult part is now over for me, and my final years will be successful with minimal difficulty.

I like being able to read my chart and have a good idea what potentials lay in store for me. You will, too, when you learn to read your own chart after reading this book.

By now, you should be able to get some idea of the value and the fun of astrology.

SATURN

Saturn is the "teacher" planet and the planet of perfect justice. Through Saturn's influence we learn, but not always easily. And Saturn lets us reap what we sow. If you sow good seed (good works) Saturn assures reward. Of course, if you sow bad seed, watch out! You will get exactly what you deserve.

Many astrologers consider Saturn to be a malefic planet because it is associated with obstacles, difficulties, hardships, working to earn rather than getting a free ride.

Let me digress for a moment. Traditional astrology considers Mars, Saturn, Uranus, and Pluto to be malefic planets. The Sun, Moon, Venus, and Jupiter are considered to be benefic planets. Mercury and Neptune are considered to be neutral. I do not subscribe to this philosopy.

The so-called malefic planets are often associated with difficulties, but I do not consider this to be bad (malefic). Difficulties give us the opportunity to develop character and strength. If you want a sharp knife, you must put it to the grindstone. If you want a strong character, you must go through tests and difficulties (life's grindstone).

The so-called benefic planets are often associated with easy going (little or no difficulties), but I do not consider this to necessarily be good (benefic). Too much ease in a chart never gives the person the character development he/she needs. For example, the rich kid who has everything given to him from birth on, and grows up to be a incapable of doing anything worthwhile.

And I do not believe any planet is neutral.

My philosophy is that it is the choices the person makes with regard to their planetary influences that determines good, bad, or neutral. For example, Saturn may present a certain difficulty in a person's chart. That person can choose to give up and become a failure or to overcome and become a success. The planets present the circumstances and options, the person makes the choices.

Now back to Saturn. I'll not mention malefic or benefic again in this book.

In general, Saturn functions more powerfully in Capricorn, Libra, and Virgo.

In general, Saturn functions with more difficulty in Cancer, Aries, and Pisces.

In the other six signs (Taurus, Gemini, Leo, Scorpio, Sagittarius, and Aquarius), it seems to hit a happy medium between easy and difficult.

Saturnian types tend to be: serious, sincere, cautious, conventional, judicious.

Some positive influences of Saturn are: stability, self-discipline, wisdom, thriftiness, patience, endurance, humility.

Some negative influences of Saturn can make one: miserly, narrow-minded, selfish, fearful, pessimistic, and not flexible (rigid).

Saturn rules Capricorn. It also rules the body skeleton, teeth, skin, knees, paralysis, fear, falls, chronic conditions, calcium, gall bladder.

Saturn moves through all twelve zodiac signs in approximately 29 1/2 years, staying in one sign an average of 2 1/2 years.

Saturn travels from 0 degrees to 8 minutes a day, depending on whether it is in retrograde or direct motion.

Figure 1 shows that my Saturn is in Sagittarius in the 4th house. This placement shows that my father was a strict disciplinarian, which he was. Saturn represents the father in a chart (the Moon, the mother) and the 4th house is the domestic scene; Saturn is the disciplinarian.

Saturn's house placement shows the area of a person's life where that person has the most lessons to learn and where the person has the greatest feeling of inadequacy.

URANUS

Uranus is associated with sudden changes and events for which there is no warning. The circumstances that turn your life completely around in an instant are Uranean events. Uranus in a horoscope is rarely subtle. It brings excitement and change whether you want it or not.

Sometimes Uranus merely describes where there is a strong desire to be free or unconventional. It is also associated with rebellious urges.

Uranus is related to intuitive and psychic ability and events. If you tune into the Uranus energies, you can develop your latent creative abilities.

A strong Uranus in a chart indicates a person who is unconventional, original, intuitive, and individualistic.

Uranus is also the planet of divorce and separation.

Uranus sometimes denotes extensive power or the desire for great power on the part of the person involved. This is especially true if Uranus is in aspect with the Sun or with Leo in a natal chart.

Uranus rules astrology, electricity, astronauts, body spasms or other body problems related to malfunctioning of the body electricity, the new and unusual, lightning, inventions, friends, and government officials.

Uranus is the planet associated with mental and spiritual awakening and enlightenment,

In general, Uranus functions more powerfully in Aquarius, Scorpio, Gemini, and Libra.

In general, Uranus functions with more difficulty in Leo, Taurus, Sagittarius, and Aries.

In the other four signs (Cancer, Virgo, Capricorn, and Pisces), it seems to hit a happy medium between easy and difficult.

Uranus rules occult activities and metaphysics, independent thinking, impulsive energy, reformers, non-conformists, change.

Some positive characteristics associated with Uranus's influence include: clairvoyance, strength of will, intuition, humanitarian ideals, magnetism and resource- fulness.

Some negative Uranus characteristics are: rebellious- ness, fanaticism, a dictatorial or a radical nature; eccentric- ity, and perversion.

Uranus rules Aquarius. It also rules the lower legs and ankles, tension, nervous conditions, blood circula- tion, x-rays, the intuitive mind.

Uranus moves through all twelve zodiac signs in ap- proximately 84 years, staying in one sign an average of 7 years.

Uranus travels from 0 degrees to 4 minutes a day, de- pending on whether it is in retrograde or direct motion.

Figure 1 shows that my Uranus is in Aries in the 8th house. This position indicates that my death will be sud- den. No lingering illnesses for me.

Because of aspects to my Sun, Pluto, and Moon, a great many other things are also indicated, which we will discuss later when we delve more deeply into chart inter- pretation.

NEPTUNE

Neptune is the most difficult planet to describe be- cause it rules anything that is difficult to pin down, define, clarify in specific terms.

Perhaps the best way to give you an idea of what Neptune is all about is to list some of the things it rules: mysterious events, psychic matters, drugs, poisons, hos- pitals, institutions, illusions, hypnosis, magic, fraud, chaos, comas, confusion, dreams, mystical matters, inde- cision, secrets, illusive problems, extreme sensitivity.

When Neptune is well aspected in a chart, it can signify great good fortune and protection that seems almost supernatural.

The Neptune influence on a person can bring great devotion or even the urge to martyrdom.

Persons with a strong Neptune in their chart often appear to be dreamy or to be frequently living in some other dimension.

The higher vibrations of Neptune are spiritual, psychic, compassionate, understanding, self-sacrificing, and imaginative.

The lower vibrations of Neptune are feelings of powerlessness, sorrows, delusion, misplaced sympathies, and fraudulent conditions.

In general, Neptune functions more powerfully in Pisces, Sagittarius, and Cancer.

In general, Neptune functions with more difficulty in Virgo, Gemini, and Capricorn.

In the other six signs (Aries, Taurus, Leo, Libra, Scorpio, and Aquarius), it seems to hit a happy medium between easy and difficult.

Neptunian types tend to be: psychic, idealistic, creative, sensitive, impressionable, musical.

Some positive characteristics of Neptune's influence are: mystic experiences, especially clairvoyance; inspiration, genius, devotion, reverence.

Some negative Neptune characteristics are: self-indulgence, chaotic events, immorality, negativity, black magic, delusion.

Neptune rules Pisces. It also rules feet and toes, toxic conditions, leakage (especially water), malformations, anything that is difficult to pin down.

Neptune moves through all twelve zodiac signs in approximately 165 years, staying in one sign approximately 14 years.

Neptune travels from 0 degrees to 3 minutes a day, depending on whether it is in retrograde or direct motion.

Figure 1 shows that my Neptune is in Leo in the 1st house. This is an extremely powerful placement in my chart, and we will discuss it in length later.

For now, make note that Neptune rules hypnosis, and the first house rules the person's body, character, and personality. Here are a couple facts about me: I am a certified hypnotherapist and have written two books about hypnosis.

See the connection?

PLUTO

The announcement of Pluto's discovery was made on March 12, 1930. There is much about Pluto that is not yet known or certain simply because there has not been sufficient time to study it. All the other planets have had hundreds of years of study. It takes Pluto 248 years to travel through all twelve zodiac signs. At this writing, we have only been able to study and observe it through the last half of Cancer, all through Leo, Virgo, and Libra, and through the early degrees of Scorpio. What does seem evident is that the sign Pluto affects entire generations of people and is not specifically significant in individual natal charts.

However, the house placement and the aspects it makes with other planets are quite significant in individual natal charts. Pluto, like Uranus and Neptune, can attract psychic experiences when strongly linked with other planets.

A very strong Pluto in a chart generally indicates an outstanding person. This person will most likely be a nonconformist who brings new developments into the world. It can also indicate great amounts of money and power behind the scenes for the person.

Pluto is the great transformer. It breaks down the old, and replaces it with the new. Pluto is associated with the most drastic changes, forced conditions, mass movements.

In mythology, Pluto ruled the underworld and was the first kidnapper. It was discovered in the thirties when kidnapping ran rampant (e.g., the Lindberg kidnapping), when crime, gangsters, and racketeering (Al Capone) flourished, and the "underworld" became very powerful. Also dictators (Hitler, Mussolini, Stalin and others) emerged into world prominence. Pluto rules all of these things.

Labor strikes involving masses of people also fall under the domain of Pluto. Mass production in industry, also. The list of these sorts of things is quite extensive. Pluto is no small-time influence.

On a more personal basis, Pluto rules work behind the scenes or in isolation, death and disappearances, retirement, urge to tear down and rebuild, influences sexual behavior, and secret obsessions.

In general, Pluto functions more powerfully in Scorpio and Aquarius. In general, Pluto functions with more difficulty in Taurus and Leo.

In the remaining eight signs not enough is known to make knowledgeable statements about Pluto's functioning with regard to easy or difficult.

Some basic Pluto characteristics are: extrasensory perception, forcefulness, intensity, restructuring.

Some positive Pluto characteristics are: spirituality, transformation and revitalization, positive clairvoyance.

Some negative Pluto characteristics are: destruction, fanaticism, anarchy, atrocities.

Pluto rules Scorpio. It also rules the reproductive organs, rectum, obsessions, deep-seated problems, the prostate gland, and allergies.

Pluto moves through all twelve zodiac signs in approximately 248 years, staying in one sign from 14 to 30 years.

Pluto travels from 0 degrees to 3 minutes a day, depending on whether it is in retrograde or direct motion.

Figure 1 shows that my Pluto is in Cancer in the 11th house. This house placement shows that I will deal with masses of people, which is exactly what I do as an author of books.

NODES OF THE MOON

The nodes of the Moon are not planets. There is a north node and a south node; they are calculated points in space based on the Moon's position. The position of the north node is indicated in the Ephemeris (refer to figure 3 to refresh your recollection). The south node is always exactly opposite the north node. The nodes are always in retrograde motion.

We have a solar eclipse when both the Sun and Moon are exactly conjunct either of the nodes. We have a lunar eclipse when the Sun and Moon are in exact opposition and accompanied by the nodes.

The reason I include the nodes in this chapter on planets is because their influence can be interpreted as though they were planets. In my opinion, it is a minor influence and I usually do not bother to interpret them in a natal analysis unless the chart is so lacking in major aspects that I need to use all I can get. Other astrologers might disagree with my stance. When you start doing your own chart interpretations, use your own judgement.

Traditionally, the north node is viewed to have an influence somewhat like that of the planet Jupiter. The south node is viewed to be somewhat like Saturn.

The north node in a chart represents the area where development of new talents should be directed.

The south node in a chart represents talents already developed. My north node is in Taurus in my 9th house conjunct my midheaven, and my south node is in Scorpio conjunct my nadir (refer to figure 1). I would interpret this to mean that I should concentrate on earning money (Taurus) in publishing (9th house) because my writing ability (3rd house) is already developed. I should write about occult matters (Scorpio) which I already know. This, in fact, is exactly what I now do.

The nodes seem to have some association with the subconscious mind. Some astrologers regard the nodes to be karmic points or fated conditions. In experience, I have not encountered any evidence from which to draw my own conclusion about this karmic or fated aspect.

I try to keep an open mind, and I urge you to do the same. Enough said about the nodes.

PART OF FORTUNE

Like the nodes, the Part of Fortune is not a planet; it is a calculated point in space that can be interpreted as though it were a planet.

The Part of Fortune is said to be a lucky point.

If you will look at figure 1 near the bottom center you will see: PART OF FORTUNE = 25CN11, which is the location of my Part of Fortune.

When I study the cosmic events in my life associated with good luck, sometimes the Part of Fortune has been involved and sometimes not. In any case, I regard this as such a minor influence that I do not bother to calculate it or interpret it.

When you use computer calculated charts like I now do, you get the Part of Fortune for free. If you do the same, you may want to keep an eye on it to see if it is significant in your natal chart.

I would interpret my placement as being lucky in my dealings with masses of people (11th house) especially with regard to domestic or psychic matters (Cancer).

Enough said about the Part of Fortune.

SUMMARY

This has been a brief discussion of the planets' salient points. It is by no means an exhaustive presentation of facts. I could easily written four times as much on each planet and still not have covered everything.

My purpose is not to deluge you will large amounts of data. My purpose is to give you a sufficient amount of key, salient information so you can begin to understand and use astrology. For those readers who want to know more, there are literally hundreds of books available for further study.

In this chapter, I also exposed you to mini-analysis and interpretations to better prepare you for a more thorough discussion on these matters later in this book.

By seeing how one natal chart, mine, is constructed and interpreted you will be able to do the same thing with your own chart (or other people's charts).

6

The Aspects

Aspects have now been mentioned dozens of times in this book, and you are probably getting a fairly good idea of their importance in natal chart interpretation. Later in the book when I specifically discuss analysis and interpretation, I will spend a great deal of time discussing aspects.

For now, I want to give you just a little broader, but brief, view of aspects.

I will cover both major and minor aspects here to give you a well rounded knowledge, but I will not discuss the minor aspects in any detail later.

CONJUNCTION

This is a major aspect where two planets are within 8 degrees of each other. If they are less than one degree apart, they are considered to be exactly conjunct, and this is when it is the most powerful.

Depending on the two planets involved, the conjunction may be harmonious (easy) or inharmonious (difficult).

The keywords for a conjunction are PROMINENCE

and INTENSITY because each planet in a conjunction tends to bring out the characteristics of the other planet involved. In other words, the two planets mutually intensify each other.

"Mutually intensify" applies only to conjunctions, and it means that the planets involved have much more power and influence in the horoscope than if they were not conjunct (or "conjoined") because their powers combine, generally in a beneficial way but not always.

The conjunction might enhance the mutual attributes. For example: Mercury conjunct Mars will give an exceptionally keen, active mind.

A conjunction can sometimes have a compromising effect. For example: Saturn conjunct Jupiter. Saturn tends to restrict Jupiter's expansiveness, and Jupiter tends to free the Saturn restrictiveness. As a result, there is a compromise—less hardship than Saturn would normally bring and less good fortune than Jupiter would normally bring.

An example of a very powerful, intense conjunction can be found in figure 1 in the 1st house. My Neptune at 29LE23 is only 43 minutes away from my Mars at 00VI06. You can find the effects of this conjunction in chapter 13. This is an example of two planets being conjunct even though they are in different signs. This is possible because Neptune is only 37 minutes away from being at zero degrees Virgo. Do you see how to figure this?

$$
\begin{array}{r}
29 \quad \text{LE} \quad 23 \\
+ \quad\quad\quad 37 \\
\hline
29 \quad\quad 60 \quad = \quad 00 \quad \text{VI} \quad 00
\end{array}
$$

If you don't see this, refer back to chapter 3 where the degrees and seconds of signs are discussed. Recall that there are 30 degrees to each sign: 0 degrees through 29 degrees 59 minutes make up any one sign. If you add one minute more, it becomes 0 degrees of the next sign.

Another conjunction in figure 1 is in the 11th house. My Sun at 12CN05 is 5 degrees and 40 minutes away from my Pluto at 17CN45. This meets the criteria of being within 8 degrees of each other and thus qualifies as a conjunction. However, at nearly 6 degrees apart, it is only a moderately powerful conjunction. It lacks the intensity of the Neptune-Mars conjunction just discussed.

Some other conjunctions in figure 1 are:

In 10th house, Jupiter at 04GE51 is 4 degrees 21 minutes from Moon at 09GE42. Fairly strong.

In 10th house, Venus at 26TA31 is 8 degrees 20 minutes from Jupiter at 04GE51. This is a weak conjunction because it is on the fringe of not being a conjunction. Not much intensity.

See if you can find these additional conjunctions in figure 1: Venus conjunct the midheaven; Neptune conjunct the ascendant; Mars conjunct the ascendant; north node conjunct the midheaven; north node conjunct Venus.

Conjunctions add a great deal of strength to any natal chart.

TRINE

This is a major aspect where two planets are 120 degrees apart, plus or minus 8 degrees (that is from 112 to 128 degrees apart). Of course, the more exact, the more powerful the influence.

The trine is a very powerful aspect, and it is always harmonious (easy). Trines in a chart help the person to overcome difficulties in life and sometimes bring great good fortune.

The keyword for the trine is EASY LUCK. The trine indicates where things come with little effort for the person. It identifies natural talents and where success is most easily obtained.

An example of a trine can be found in figure 1. Neptune in the 1st house at 29LE23 is 3 degrees 18 minutes from being exactly 120 degrees from Saturn in the 4th house at 26SA06. This is a fairly strong trine.

Some other trines in figure 1 are: Mars trine Saturn; Saturn trine the ascendant.

Occasionally in a horoscope chart you will see three planets, each of which forms a trine with the other two. This is called a Grand Trine, and it is extremely powerful for good. The meanings of each of the three trines in a grand trine is the same as each trine separately. However, in the Grand Trine configuration, the power is increased many times, and it will overcome all, or nearly all, inharmonious aspects that may be in the horoscope chart.

SEXTILE

This is a major aspect where two planets are 60 degrees apart, plus or minus 8 degrees (52 to 68 degrees apart). This is always a harmonious aspect, but not as powerful as a trine. The keyword for a sextile is OPPORTUNITY.

Sextiles show where there is opportunity and luck through action. For the sextile to bring the luck or results, you must take action, usually work, for it. Conversely, the trine most often gives you the good luck with little or no action on your part.

An example of a sextile in figure 1 is the Moon sextile Uranus. This is quite a strong sextile because they are within 1 degree and 37 minutes of being exactly 60 degrees apart.

Some other sextiles in figure 1 are: Pluto sextile the north node; Pluto sextile the midheaven.

SQUARE

This is a major aspect where two planets are 90 degrees apart, plus or minus 8 degrees (82 to 98 degrees apart). This is a very powerful aspect, and is the most difficult and potentially destructive of all aspects. The keyword for the square is OBSTACLES.

Squares put lots of energy into the chart and keep you very busy overcoming obstacles. If you learn to use this energy constructively, squares are quite beneficial. Otherwise, they can hold you back or beat you down. The effect of squares depends entirely on your attitude. If you are a negative person, a lot of squares in your chart can make life a living hell.

Squares in a chart indicate where you will feel compelled to strive harder and where you are most likely to have clashes.

I have analyzed hundreds of charts, and I have never seen a chart of an outstanding person without also seeing more than one square in the chart. Squares are absolutely necessary to develop character. The key is to use the energy from the squares in a positive, constructive manner.

I have seen several charts that had no squares at all. In every case, the people involved drifted through life without even the smallest achievement. They seemed contented because life had not handed them any significant problems, but it had not handed them any significant rewards either.

You can see why I do not regard squares as being "the bad boys of astrology" as do some astrologers. I firmly believe we need challenges, obstacles, and problems in order to get the most out of life. Squares give those things to you.

An example of a square can be found in figure 1. My Sun at 12CN05 in the 11th house is within 46 seconds of being an exact square to my Uranus at 11AR19 in the 8th house. This is an extremely strong square.

Some other squares in figure 1 are: Uranus square Pluto; Venus square Mars; Venus square Neptune; Mars square Jupiter; Jupiter square Neptune; Venus square ascendant.

Once in a great while in a horoscope chart you will see four planets, each of which forms a square with two of the other planets and an opposition with the third. This is called a Grand Square, and it is extremely powerful. It gives a great many obstacles in the person's life. Each square and the oppositions are interpreted just the same as though they were single, but the grand square configuration increases the power many times. It takes a tremendous amount of work and fortitude to overcome the difficulties presented by a grand square. Many people are defeated or held back by this configuration. Those who learn to flow with the energy and redirect it into a positive direction will become outstanding individuals.

OPPOSITION

This is a major aspect where two planets are 180 degrees apart, plus or minus 8 degrees (172 to 188 degrees). This is a difficult aspect, but not as much as is the square. The keywords for the opposition are COOPERATION or AWARENESS.

The opposition indicates areas where there is need to balance opposing forces or circumstances to find a happy medium. There is always a certain amount of difficulty in doing this. Many adjustments have to be made in order to make best use of the energies created by oppositions.

Through the confrontations caused by oppositions, you have the opportunity to gain greater awareness of self and of others.

Opposition creates pushing and pulling in ones life, and only by learning to cooperate can this be resolved satisfactorily.

In figure 1 there is an example of an opposition. My Mercury at 2OGE42 in the 10th house is in opposition to my Saturn at 26SA25 in the 4th house. This opposition is 5 degrees 24 minutes from being exact and is only moderately strong. Basically it tells me that I need to learn to discipline my mind. Since it is not a strong aspect in my chart, that was not a big problem for me—although it was one that I did face, and solve many years ago when I was much younger.

There are no other oppositions in my chart.

SEMI-SEXTILE

This is a minor aspect where two planets are 30 degrees apart, plus or minus 3 degrees (27 to 33 degrees apart). The keyword for the semi-sextile is COOPERATIVE.

The sextile is much like the sextile, but it is considerably less powerful.

There are a number of semi-sextiles in figure 1. One of them is the Sun-Moon, which are 32 degrees 23 minutes apart. A fairly weak aspect.

SEMI-SQUARE

This is a minor aspect where two planets are 45 degrees apart, plus or minus 3 degrees (42 to 48 apart). The keyword for the semi-square is FRICTION.

The semi-square is much like the square, but it is considerably less powerful. It is a minor frustrating aspect.

There are several semi-squares in figure 1. One of them is Venus-Sun, which are 34 seconds from being exact, a strong semi-square aspect.

SESQUI-SQUARE

This is a minor aspect where two planets are 135 degrees apart, plus or minus 3 degrees (132 to 138 degrees apart). The keyword for the sesqui-square is AGITATION. It introduces minor obstacles that are an agitation more than a serious problem.

There is only one sesqui-square in figure 1, and that is between Uranus and the ascendant, which are 1 degree 14 seconds from being exact. This is just a moderately strong aspect.

INCONJUNCT or QUINCUNX

This is a minor aspect where two planets are 150 degrees apart, plus or minus 3 degrees (147 to 153 degrees apart). The keyword for the inconjunct is GROWTH.

This is probably the most important of the minor aspects, and is probably one worth watching in natal charts.

This aspect indicates problems you need to learn to adapt to or work around, which can lead to maturity and increased self-confidence (growth). This aspect can be harsh or easy, depending on the specific planets involved. If the ascendant is involved, it can indicate health problems.

There is only one inconjunct in figure 1, and that is between Venus and Saturn, which are only 25 seconds from being exact. This is a very strong inconjunct, and I felt its influence for a number of years until I learned how to apportion my time and energies satisfactorily between my home life and my work life. Once I found the right balance and attitude, the inconjunct was no longer apparent.

In this inconjunct, Saturn represents my work life (Saturn rules work, and is also the natural ruler of the 10th house). Venus represents my wife, hence my home life.

In addition, Venus is placed in the 10th house of my public work life, and Saturn, which rules the work life is placed in my 4th house (rules the domestic scene). Everything ties together; these were the areas I needed to adapt my behavior to in order to solve conflicting problems.

7

The Houses

Every possible aspect of a person's life is ruled by one of the houses. Therefore, the twelve houses of a natal chart depict the entire life of the person in every respect.

In this book, I will not even come close to delineating all of the factors ruled by each house. The list would be unreasonably long, and most of the items would not be of any great interest anyway. For example, who really cares to find out about the long journeys of their sister-in-law? This is one of the many things that falls under the 5th house rulership, and it is the kind of thing that will not be discussed here.

What I will list for each house are those principal items that concern most people most of the time. You are interested in your health, love, children, travels, work, etc. and this is what I shall restrict my discussion to.

KINDS OF HOUSES

Angular:

These are the 1st, 4th, 7th, and 10th houses. Planets placed in these houses have a greater scope of action than planets placed in other houses.

When the majority of planets in a person's natal chart are in angular houses, it indicates a prominent position in the world.

> 1st: Personal character
> 4th: Latter part of life
> 7th: Fortune of marriage
> 10th: Public recognition

If you look at figure 1, you will see a portion of the chart at the bottom labeled HOUSES. It shows seven planets in angular (ANG) houses; two in the 1st, one in the 4th, and four in the 10th. The overwhelming majority of planets in my chart are in angular houses.

Succedent:

These are the 2nd, 5th, 8th, and 11th houses. Planets placed in these houses tend to give stability, willpower, fixity of purpose, but no great activity.

When the majority of planets in a person's natal chart are in succedent houses, it indicates the person may be stubborn and uncompromising.

Figure 1 shows I have three planets in succedent (SUC) houses: one in the 8th and two in the 11th.

Cadent:

These are the 3rd, 6th, 9th, and 12th houses. Planets placed in these houses generally express very little activity. They tend toward thought, communication of ideas, and the ability to get along with people.

When the majority of planets in a person's natal chart are in cadent houses, there is usually very little, if any, public recognition. The person will probably complete a major part of any undertaking, but someone else will get the credit.

Figure 1 shows that I do not have any planets in cadent (CAD) houses.

HOUSES OF FUNCTION

Houses of Life:
These are the 1st, 5th, and 9th houses. These are houses of dynamic energy, enthusiasm, motivating power, religious conviction. The 1st is self; 5th children; 9th philosophy of living. These houses are the fire triplicity.

Houses of Endings:
These are the 4th, 8th, and 12th houses. The 4th house pictures the end of life or the end of a matter. The 8th house pictures death and regeneration. The 12th house pictures the subconscious, karma, and what is brought into this life. These houses are the water triplicity.

Houses of Substances:
These are the 2nd, 6th, and 10th houses. The 2nd house depicts the accumulation of money and movable possessions. The 6th house depicts the facility to work or the occupation. The 10th house depicts the employer or profession, reputation, and honors. These houses are the earth triplicity.

Houses of Relationships:
These are the 3rd, 7th, and 11th houses. These describe the person's relationship in the community as follows: The 3rd house describes relationships with relatives and neighbors; the 7th house describes relationships with partners (marriage and business); the 11th house describes relationships with friends and organizations. These houses are the air triplicity.

THE TWELVE HOUSES

FIRST HOUSE

Persons in the First House: You, the self, your body.
Matters of the First House: The beginning, self-interest, the present, early environment.
Key First House Rulerships:
1. The head and face.
2. Your physical body and its appearance, including stature, complexion, attractiveness, strength, energy, constitution, abnormalities (if any), grace and poise (or awkwardness), coordination, physical desires, etc. In short, everything concerning your physical body.
3. Your personal affairs (not sexual affairs).
4. Your personality.
5. Your attitude and outlook on life.
6. The impression you make on others. That is, how others see you.
7. Your personal environment.
8. Your private life.
9. Self-awareness.

A Few Occupations: Soldiers, explorers, pioneers.

SECOND HOUSE

Persons in the Second House: Bankers, investors, all persons who deal with money.
Matters of the Second House: Money, personal freedom, movable possessions, acquisitions.
Key Second House Rulerships:
1. The neck, throat, and base of skull.

2. Self-preservation.
3. Self-earned or self-acquired money and possessions.
4. Your money, finances, securities, movable goods, holdings, etc.
5. Borrowing and lending.
6. Penalties and fines.
7. Financial gains.
8. How you receive and give.

A Few Occupations: Stockbrokers, bankers, accountants.

THIRD HOUSE

Persons in the Third House: Brothers, sisters, neighbors.
Matters of the Third House: Communications, short trips, the conscious mind.
Key Third House Rulerships:
1. The arms, wrists, hands, fingers, shoulders, lungs, thyroid gland and nervous system.
2. Your brothers, sisters, and neighbors.
3. Your mentality, how your mind functions.
4. Your nervous energy.
5. Your will power.
6. Transportation.

A Few Occupations: Writers, speakers, salespersons, radio announcers, teachers, auctioneers, reporters, secretaries.

FOURTH HOUSE

Persons in the Fourth House: Parent, provider, patron.
Matters of the Fourth House: House and home, land, domestic affairs, end of life, end of a matter.

Key Fourth House Rulerships:
1. The stomach, digestive system, ribs, breasts.
2. Your home, domestic environment.
3. Land, immovable possessions, property, mines.
4. Parent of your opposite sex.
5. The end of your life.
6. The end of matters (for example, the end of a love affair or the end of a job).
7. Your grave (final resting place).
8. Your sense of security.
9. Circumstances in your later life.
10. Your base of operations.

A Few Occupations: Cooks and chefs, butlers and maids, nutritionists, miners.

FIFTH HOUSE

Persons in the Fifth House: Child, lover, entertainer, gambler.

Matters of the Fifth House: Love affairs, children, talent, speculation, entertainment, gambling, sports.

Key Fifth House Rulerships:
1. The heart.
2. Your love affairs (not sexual affairs).
3. Your children.
4. Sports.
5. Hobbies.
6. Relaxation and entertainment.
7. Gambling and speculation.
8. Education.
9. Games of all sorts.
10. Creative urges.
11. Ego to leave something of yourself behind when you die.

12. Theaters and other places of entertainment.

A Few Occupations: Actors and actresses, professional entertainers in general, professional athletes, artists.

SIXTH HOUSE

Persons in the Sixth House: Workers, doctors, nurses, landlords.

Matters of the Sixth House: Illness, employment, service, labor.

Key Sixth House Rulerships:
1. The intestines.
2. Conditions under which you work.
3. Your general state of health.
4. Your employees, subordinates, etc.
5. Your suseptibility to illness.
6. The service you are capable of giving.
7. Disagreeable duties and work.
8. Clothing.
9. Diet.
10. Small animals, both domestic and wild.
11. Love of animals.
12. The manner in which you perform your obligations.
13. Labor and work in general.
14. Tools used for performing work.

A Few Occupations: Physicians, nurses, health practitioners and those in the health care field in general.

SEVENTH HOUSE

Persons in the Seventh House: Spouse, partners, the public, enemies.

Matters of the Seventh House: Marriage, divorce, partnerships, the public.

Key Seventh House Rulerships:
1. Kidneys, bladder, groin.
2. Marriage and partnership.
3. Describes your spouse.
4. Success or failures in marriage and partnerships.
5. Your public or open enemies.
6. Sexual perverseness.
7. Your dealings with others in general.
8. Your social drive.
9. Your awareness of others.

A Few Occupations: Judges, referees and umpires.

EIGHTH HOUSE

Persons in the Eighth House: Investigators, persons dealing with the dead and affairs of the dead.

Matters of the Eighth House: Other people's money, surgery, manner of death, regeneration.

Key Eighth House Rulerships:
1. Sex organs, rectum, urethra
2. Veneral diseases.
3. Sex drive.
4. Cause of your death.
5. Affairs of the dead in general (for example, inheritance, wills, life insurance, funerals).
6. Whether you will profit or lose through another's death.
7. Slaughter houses.
8. Surgery and autopsies.
9. Morgues.
10. Other people's money.
11. Some occult experiences.

A Few Occupations: Butchers, morticians, executioners, detectives, pathologists, any occupation connected with death.

NINTH HOUSE

Persons in the Ninth House: Strangers, publishers, clergy, diplomats.

Matter of the Ninth House: Long journeys, printing and publishing, law, courts, philosophy, religion, foreign affairs and matters, higher education.

Key Ninth House Rulerships:
1. Hips, thighs, buttocks, the sciatic nerve.
2. Religion and related activities.
3. Your philosophy, beliefs and spiritual leanings.
4. The courts, law, and the legal system.
5. Some psychic experiences.
6. Higher education.
7. Long trips and travel to foreign countries.
8. Large animals, both domestic and wild.
9. Places far away from your birthplace.
10. Church.
11. Higher thoughts, expanding consciousness.

A Few Occupations: Lawyers, clergy, diplomats, printers, publishers, bookbinders.

TENTH HOUSE

Persons in the Tenth House: Employer, parent, president, head person (the one in charge).

Matters of the Tenth House: Career, reputation, activity, honors.

Key Tenth House Rulerships:

1. The joints, knees, skeletal structure, teeth.
2. Your public life (this is the most public house).
3. Your true profession, business, vocation, or means of earning a living.
4. Your ambition.
5. How the public views you.
6. Your reputation, any honors or recognition you gain.
7. Rewards of karma.
8. Your standing in the community.
9. Your parent of the same sex.
10. Persons in power (presidents, officials, kings).
11. Your goals, aspirations, achievements, promotions.
12. Business.
13. Your authority.

A Few Occupations: Politicians, business leaders, managers, directors, any position of leadership or power.

ELEVENTH HOUSE

Persons in the Eleventh House: Friends, social contacts, the public at large, advisors.

Matters of the Eleventh House: Hopes, wishes, friends, groups, organizations.

Key Eleventh House Rulerships:

1. The ankles and calves.
2. Your hopes and wishes.
3. Your likes and dislikes.
4. Your friends.
5. Idealism.
6. How you interact with masses of people.
7. Clubs and organizations, especially those of a humanitarian nature.
8. Your ability to overcome obstacles.

9. Your reputation in money matters and as a winner.
10. Any sort of organization to which you belong.

A Few Occupations: Any humanitarian work.

TWELFTH HOUSE

Persons in the Twelfth House: Widows, orphans, secret enemies.

Matters of the Twelfth House: Institutions, escapism, self-undoing, subversion, subconscious.

Key Twelfth House Rulerships:
1. The feet and toes, phlegm and mucus.
2. Self-undoing, downfall, bad habits.
3. Prisons.
4. Hospitals.
5. Secrets.
6. Secret enemies.
7. Work or activity behind the scenes.
8. Confinements in institutions.
9. Limitations, restraints, restrictions of all sorts.
10. The hidden side of your life.
11. Crime.
12. Misfortune, trouble, losses, pain, sorrow, etc.
13. Your most difficult tasks and hardest battles.
14. Things you must work out for yourself.
15. Fierce animals that could cause you harm.

A Few Occupations: Wardens, prison guards, spies, thieves.

PART II

ERECTING
A
NATAL CHART

8

The Modern Way— By Computer

There are three ways to compile a natal chart: by computer, which will be discussed in this chapter; by "eyeballing," which will be discussed in chapter 9; by hand calculated math, which will be discussed in chapter 10.

Each method has its advantages and disadvantages. You can evaluate each, and choose the one, or ones, you prefer. I have used all three extensively, and I prefer the computer generated charts by far over the other two.

By now you know what a computer generated natal chart looks like because you have referred to figure 1 dozens of times up to this point in the book.

Figure 4 is another computer generated chart, my wife's, which I am including now because it shows an important feature that I have deliberately not mentioned before.

Figure 4 illustrates a natal chart with intercepted signs. Until now, we have discussed charts that have a different zodiac sign on each house cusp. That is, twelve houses, each with a different zodiac sign ruling it.

A chart with intercepted signs has some duplicated

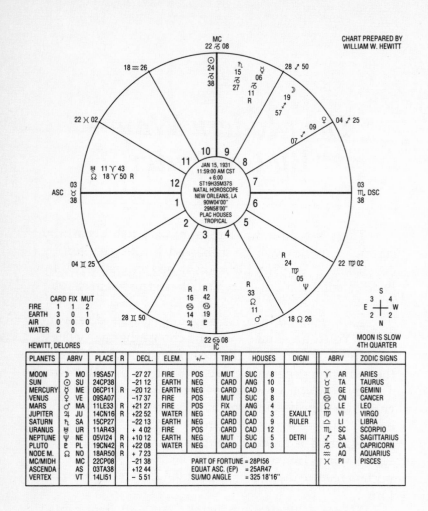

Figure 4
Natal Chart with Intercepted Signs.

signs on house cusps and has other signs that do not appear on any house cusp. The signs that do not appear on any house cusp are contained completely within some house—they are "intercepted" in that house.

Look at figure 4, and I'll explain. Look at the Ascendant (ASC); it has Taurus on the 1st house cusp.

Going counterclockwise, look at the cusp of the second house. It has Gemini on it. Look at the 3rd house; it also has Gemini on it.

Follow the house cusps around. When you get to the 6th house, notice that it has Virgo, but when you proceed to the 7th, it has Scorpio. What happened to Libra which comes between Virgo and Scorpio?

Libra falls completely within, or is intercepted by, the 6th house. The 6th house is a really big house in this chart, having approximately 41 degrees in it.

The 12th house on the opposite side of the chart also has 41 degrees in it because Aries is completely contained (intercepted) in the 12th house.

In this chart then, the 2nd and 3rd houses are each ruled by Gemini, the 8th and 9th houses are each ruled by Sagittarius, and Libra and Aries are intercepted by the 6th and 12 houses respectively.

This is what is meant by a natal chart with intercepted signs. Sometimes you will hear the term "captured signs," which means the same thing as intercepted signs.

So what is the big deal about charts with intercepted signs? Not much, really. You interpret them just the same as any other chart; all the same rules apply. But you need to be aware of what they are, otherwise you would think there was an error when you cast a chart with intercepted signs.

Intercepted signs are fairly common, and occur mostly in charts for extreme northern or southern locations, although they can occur anywhere. Notice my chart in figure 1 is for Toledo, Ohio, and the one for my wife in figure 4 is considerably further south, New Orleans.

Even though I am discussing this in the chapter about computer generated charts, this information is valid for hand calculated charts also. This just happened to be the point where I decided to discuss the matter.

Now back to computer generated charts.

A glance at figure 4 shows all of the information given clearly. Not only do you get a very accurate chart wheel, you get various tables that summarize valuable information.

Also with the computer, you can generate other kinds of tables and charts such as is shown in figures 5 and 6. Figure 5 shows all the aspects and the degrees of separation. This saves much time from having to figure it out yourself. Figure 6 shows harmonic patterning, which will not be discussed in this book because it is more advanced astrology.

The advantages then of a computer generated chart are:
1. Fast to generate.
2. Get a great deal of additional information for free.
3. Extremely accurate.

With regard to accurate—the computer is accurate provided you put accurate birth information into the computer in the first place.

The facts you need to obtain an accurate chart are:
1. Month, day, and year of birth.
2. Exact time of birth, and be sure to indicate am or pm. Time of birth is usually indicated on birth certificates.
3. Place of birth (town, state, country).
4. The time zone and any time changes due to daylight savings time, war time, etc.

```
ASPECTS & 360 MIDPOINTS FOR HEWITT,WILLIAM          (GEOCENTRIC)

  MO  !  SU  !  ME  !  VE  !  MA  !  JU  !  SA  !  UR  !  NE  !  PL  !  NO  !
09GE42!12CN05!20GE42!26TA31!00VI06!04GE51!26SA06!11AR19!29GE23!17CN45!18TA30!
------+------+------+------+------+------+------+------+------+------+------+
--MO--! 32 23! 11 00! 13 11! 80 24! *CJN*!163 36! *SXT*! 79 41! 38 03! 21 12!
      !      !      !      !      ! 4 51S!      ! 1 37A!      !      !      !
25GE53!--SU--! 21 23! *SSQ*! 48 01! 37 14!164 01! *SQR*! *SSQ*! *CJN*! 53 35!
      !      !      ! 34A! !      !      !      ! 46S! 2 19A! 5 40A!      !
15GE12!01CN23!--ME--! 24 12! 69 24! 15 51! *OPP*! 69 23! 68 41! 27 03! 32 12!
      !      !      !      !      !      ! 5 24A!      !      !      !      !
03GE06!19GE18!08GE36!--VE--! *SQR*! 8 20! *INC*! *SSQ*! *SQR*! 51 14! 8 01!
      !      !      !      ! 3 35A!      ! 25S! 12S! 2 53A!      !      !
19CN54!06LE05!25CN24!13CN18!--MA--! *SQR*! *TRI*!138 47! *CJN*! *SSQ*!101 36!
      !      !      !      !      ! 4 45A! 4 00S!      ! 43S! 2 39A!      !
07GE17!23GE28!12GE47!00GE41!17CN28!--JU--!158 45! 53 32! *SQR*! *SSQ*! 16 21!
      !      !      !      !      !      !      !      ! 5 28S! 2 06S!      !
17PI54!04LI05!23PI24!11PI18!28LI06!15PI28!--SA--!105 13! *TRI*!158 21!142 24!
      !      !      !      !      !      !      !      ! 3 18S!      !      !
10TA31!26TA42!16TA01!03TA55!20GE43!08TA05!18AQ42!--UR--!138 04! *SQR*! 37 11!
      !      !      !      !      !      !      !      !      ! 6 26S!      !
19CN33!05LE44!25CN03!12CN57!29LE45!17CN07!27LI45!20GE21!--NE--! 41 38!100 54!
28GE44!14CN55!04CN14!22GE08!08LE55!26GE18!06LI55!29TA32!08LE34!--PL--! *SXT*!
      !      !      !      !      !      !      !      !      !      ! 45A!
29TA06!15GE17!04GE36!22TA30!09CN18!26TA40!07PI18!29AR54!08CN57!18GE07!--NO--!
--MC--
 18 43! 51 06! 29 44! *CJN*! 99 07! 13 52!144 53! 39 39! 98 25! *SXT*! *CJN*!
      !      !      ! 5 32A!      !      !      !      !      !      ! 2 29S!
00GE20!16GE32!05GE50!23TA45!10CN32!27TA55!08PI32!01TA09!10CN11!19GE22!19TA44!
--AS--
 77 51! *SSQ*! 66 51! *SQR*! *CJN*! 82 42! *TRI*! *SES*! *CJN*! 39 48! 99 04!
      ! 29S! !      ! 1 03S! 2 33A!      ! 1 28S! 1 14S! 1 50A!      !
18CN38!04LE49!24CN08!12CN02!28LE50!16CN12!26LI49!19GE26!28LE28!07LE39!08CN02!
------+------+------+------+------+------+------+------+------+------+------+
  MO  !  SU  !  ME  !  VE  !  MA  !  JU  !  SA  !  UR  !  NE  !  PL  !  NO  !
09GE42!12CN05!20GE42!26TA31!00VI06!04GE51!26SA06!11AR19!29LE23!17CN45!18TA30!


CHART DATA-SCOPE FOR HEWITT,WILLIAM          (HEWITT,WILLIAM          )
+---------------------------+  +---------------------------+  +-------------+
! ASPECTS PER PLANET        !  !     ASPECT ANALYSIS       !  !   HOUSES    !
!-+------+-+-------+----+---!  !-+---+------------+--------!  !-------------!
!CO!PLANET! ! DAILY  !    !  !  !NA ! ASPECT     !        !  ! PLANETS     !
!DE! NAME!R! MOTION !  # !  ! #! ME!     ARC    !  ORB   !  ! PER HOUSE   !
!-+------+-+-------+----+---!  !-+---+------------+--------!  !-----------+-!
!MO!09GE42! ! 15 01 25! 2!  ! 7!CJN!      00' ! 7 00'   !  !01=27LE33! 2!
!SU!12CN05! !    57 12! 5!  ! 1!OPP! 180 00'  ! 7 00'   !  !02=25VI24! 0!
!ME!20GE42! ! 1 01 10! 1!  ! 3!TRI! 120 00'  ! 7 00'   !  !03=23LI20! 0!
!VE!26TA31! !    59 12! 7!  ! 7!SQR!  90 00'  ! 7 00'   !  !04=20SC59! 1!
!MA!00VI06! !    35 56! 6!  ! 3!SXT!  60 00'  ! 5 00'   !  !05=00CP02! 0!
!JU!04GE51! !    12 35! 4!  ! 6!SSQ!  45 00'  ! 3 00'   !  !06=29CP51! 0!
!SA!26SA06!R!    04 15! 5!  ! 1!SES! 135 00'  ! 3 00'   !  !07=27AQ33! 0!
!UR!11AR19! !    00 36! 5!  ! 1!INC! 150 00'  ! 3 00'   !  !08=25PI24! 1!
!NE!29LE23! !    01 38! 6!  ! !   !          !        !  !09=23AR20! 1!
!PL!17CN45! !    01 34! 6!  ! !   !          !        !  !10=20TA59! 4!
!NO!18TA30!R!    00 00! 2!  !-+---+------------+--------!  !11=00CN02! 2!
!MC!20TA59! !    00 00! 3!  ! ! COPYRIGHT (C) 1982     !  !12=29CN51! 0!
!AS!27LE33! !    00 00! 6!  ! ! MATRIX SOFTWARE        !  !         ! !
+-+------+-+-------+----+---!  +---------------------------+  +-----------+-!
```

Figure 5
Computer generated chart indicating aspects
and degrees of separation.

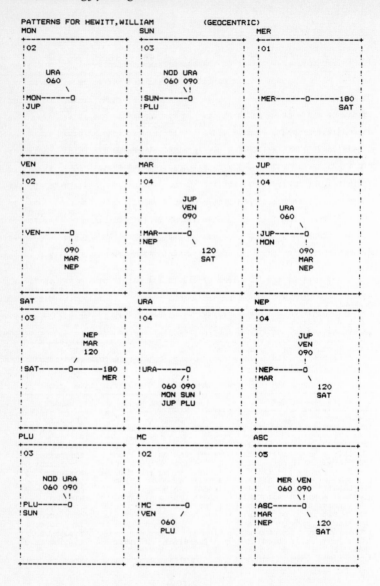

Figure 6
Computer Generated Chart: Harmonic Patterning.

If you don't know the exact time of birth, you can still obtain a reasonably accurate natal chart. Many people do not know their birth time. In these cases, *you always use a birth time of 6 am.* This provides a "solar" natal chart, which still can furnish a lot of accurate, valuable information. A solar chart will not be as complete or accurate as one cast with the exact birth time.

The computer will then do the rest of the calculations. The computer has a built in ephemeris and formulas for converting time from the ephemeris.

The ephemeris contains planet placements at Greenwich, England, which is zero longitude. Therefore, the computer must convert that to the time and place where the birth takes place, compensating for the curvature of the earth, and a few other things. It is quite complex.

The computer also figures out the house cusps by sign and degree, which is another complex process.

On my computer, this whole process for one natal chart takes approximately ten minutes. I have an older, slower computer. Newer computers would whip it out faster. By hand, it takes me several hours.

With a computer, it is also possible to have additional astrology programs that will print out a 10 - 12 page interpretation of the chart. These interpretations are pretty good, but not a substitute for a knowledgeable astrologer analyzing the chart. Figure 7 is one page from a computer interpreted chart just to give you an idea of what they are like.

The computer saves a tremendous amount of time. In a few moments I will tell you about a chart interpretation I would not have tackled without a computer because of the enormity of the job.

The computer does have disadvantages.

1. Expensive if you plan to purchase the computer and software. Even if you already have a computer, the astrology software is quite expensive.

My computer, new, was an inexpensive one at the time (1983) costing approximately $1500 for all the hardware I needed (computer, video monitor, two disk drives, a dot matrix printer, and a daisy wheel letter quality printer. The asking price for these items was nearly $3000, but I drive a hard bargain (I learned from my wife—look at her chart, and you will see it).

The software costs approximately $900 more for two programs: one to create charts, and one to print out interpretations.

The prices on the hardware and software have come down since then, but it still is expensive.

2. If you purchase the charts by mail or at a local retailer, then you must wait. Local retailers usually can furnish same day or next day service. By mail, you can wait many days or weeks. Purchasing the charts, however, is inexpensive.

For beginners, I recommend that you purchase natal charts even though you have to wait to get them. The reason is that you shouldn't spend money on the computer and software until you are sure you have a sufficient sustained interest in astrology to warrant the expense. (See the last page of the book for a special free natal chart offer.)

I created hundreds of charts by hand calculation for about 11 years before I purchased the computer. Don't wait that long!

Later in this book, I will give you information on where you can order natal charts by mail at a reasonable price.

If you live in or near a city that has a metaphysical bookstore you may discover that the bookstore has the equipment and sells natal charts.

After reading this book, weigh everything carefully and decide what is best for you.

I promised to tell you about a natal chart that I would

not have tackled if I had not had a computer.

Shortly after I purchased my computer and astrology programs I was asked by a man and his wife (previous astrology clients of mine) to help them decide the best time for their new baby to be born.

Here are the facts:

1. The baby was definitely going to be born by Caesarean section because of the mother's physical condition.

2. Their physician told them the baby could be born anytime they wished within a certain two week period he designated.

3. The only restriction was that the physician would operate only between 7 am and 10 am, Monday through Friday. This narrowed the potential birth times to 10 calendar days, and within 3 hours on any one of those days.

4. The physician agreed to make the incision at whatever time they wished in order to get the birthtime they wanted.

I had to work fast because I only had a couple days to come up with the best birth time. Of course, I asked the parents exactly what they wanted in a child, and I used that as my criteria during the ensuing investigation.

First I generated a chart for 8:30 am (the mid-point) of each day and studied those charts. I am quite good at eyeballing charts and could see the trends and changes. This enabled me to eliminate about half the days right away because of harsh aspects, full moon period, or weak aspects.

Then I zeroed in on the remaining days, generating dozens of charts, eyeballing them, making more eliminations, narrowing the time down.

Finally I had the absolute best time: 8:05 am the following Tuesday.

I also had some pretty good optional times. I discussed all options with the parents, and they went with the 8:05 on Tuesday choice.

The result: Their son was born exactly at 8:05 am. I talked again with them several years later, and they confirmed that he was exactly like I said he would be based on the astrology analysis. They said he was a perfect child. Then they asked me to do it again for their second child who was going to be born within the next couple weeks.

This was an exciting experience for me. I certainly felt that I had helped create that baby—an awesome yet humbling feeling.

Without the computer, I would not have been able to do the hundreds of calculations and compile the dozens of charts in sufficient time.

Astrology is exciting.

```
***************************************************************************
*                                                                         *
*                                                                         *
*      CHAPTER IV    AFFECTIONS * SOCIABILITY * PLEASURES * BEAUTY         *
*                                                                         *
*                                                                         *
***************************************************************************
```

K E Y   Q U A L I T Y
   YOU COUNT YOUR LOVED ONES AS YOUR OWN POSSESSIONS. ONCE COM-
MITTED TO LOVING SOMEONE OR SOMETHING, YOU STICK THROUGH THICK
AND THIN. YOU EXPRESS LOVE BY BEING AFFECTIONATE AND BY GIVING
GIFTS. YOU LOVE GOOD FOOD, SMALL AND EXPENSIVE THINGS.   VEN-TAU
K E Y   A C T I V I T Y
   BEAUTY, ART MAY BE YOUR CAREER OR BUSINESS OR ONE WHO IS IMPOR-
TANT IN YOUR LIFE HAS SUCH INTERESTS. YOU MEET THE PUBLIC WITH
SOCIAL CHARM AND WIN ATTENTION. POPULARITY THROUGH LOOKS OR PER-
SUASIVENESS. BUSINESS CONTACTS MAY TURN INTO LOVE.   VE-10TH-HSE

                    C H A P T E R   H I G H L I G H T S

***** MANY HECTIC SOCIAL, LOVE OR ARTISTIC EXPERIENCES COULD COME IN
AND OUT OF YOUR LIFE WITH GREAT RAPIDITY. UNCONVENTIONAL LOVE,
ART APPEALS TO YOU BUT MAY NOT BE VERY ENDURING. CHANGES, EX-
CITMENT, FLIRTATIONS CAN DISTURB YOUR INNER TRANQUILITY.   VE-SSQ-UR

****   YOU MAY GET CRAVINGS FOR COMFORT, SOCIAL LIFE OR SWEETS AND HAVE
FEELINGS OF DISATISFACTION WHICH ARE HARD TO APPEASE; AT TIMES
YOU MAY BE VAIN. SPOIL LOVED ONES OR HAVE VERY DIFFERENT TASTES
AND SOCIAL BACKGROUND FROM A MAN YOU LOVE OR ARE FOND OF.   SU-SSQ-VE

***   YOUR PERSONALITY IS LOVING, SWEET AND AFFECTIONATE - A BIT TOO
MUCH SO AT TIMES. YOU HAVE DESIRES ABOUT HOME, PROPERTY, FAMI-
LY WHICH ARE HARD TO SATISFY. PRETTY THINGS, LOVINGNESS AND/OR
ARTISTIC ATTAINMENTS ARE THINGS YOU STRIVE FOR.   VE-SQR-AS

**   YOU MAY IDEALIZE SOMEONE OR SOMETHING ONLY TO FIND THAT CIRCUM-
STANCES SEEM TO DENY GRATIFICATION. YOU'RE SENTIMENTAL, ROMAN-
TIC, SACRIFICIAL FOR LOVE OR ART BUT YOUR AIMS SEEM EVER OUT OF
REACH. THESE ENERGIES ARE EXCELLENT APPLIED TO CREATIVITY. VE-SQR-NE

*   YOU COULD BE VERY PURPOSEFUL IN PURSUING WHO OR WHAT YOU WANT.
YET OBSTACLES ARISE AND THE HARDER YOU TRY THE MORE FRUSTRATED
YOU MAY FEEL. A LOVED ONE SEEMS HARD TO PLEASE. KEEP A REAL-
ISTIC VIEW OF WHAT IS POSSIBLE. YOU CAN BE VERY DIPLOMATIC. VE-SQR-MA

       YOU COULD BE KNOWN FOR YOUR LOOKS. ARTISTIC ABILITY OR PUBLIC
SOCIAL EVENTS. YOU MAY DO WELL IN MODELLING, INTERIOR DECORAT-
ING, DESIGNING, THE ARTS, SELLING OR PUBLIC ENTERTAINING. THIS
ALSO APPLIES TO ANY IMPORTANT WOMAN OR SUPERIOR IN YOUR LIFE. VE-CJN-MI

       IN ONE PARTICULAR AREA OF YOUR LIFE YOU COULD BE SELF-INDULGENT.
SOCIAL ACTIVITIES AND THE LUXURIES OR GOOD THINGS IN LIFE OFTEN
COME YOUR WAY. SPOILING LOVED ONES OR YOURSELF IS FUN BUT AVOID
EXCESSIVE VANITY OR BEING EXTRAVAGANT WITH LOVED ONES.   VE-CJN-JU

Figure 7
Computer Generated Interpretation.

9

The Fast Way— By "Eyeballing"

Eyeballing is a fast, educated guess method of creating an approximation of a natal chart. It is not as accurate as a calculated chart either by computer or by hand calculation.

The advantage of eyeballing is that it is quick and does not require an expensive computer or a lot of reference books like the hand calculation method does.

The disadvantages are that an eyeballed chart lacks completeness and precise accuracy.

EYEBALLING THE PLANETS

You need an ephemeris to eyeball the planets. To show you how eyeballing works, we will use the ephemeris page in figure 3. We will use the same birth information that was used in the computerized chart in figure 1 so you can compare the results.

As a refresher the date of birth is July 4, 1929 and the time of birth is 9 am EST. For eyeballing, the place of birth is not important.

First write down the location of the planets for July 4, 1929 as shown on the ephemeris page in figure 3. This is as follows:

Sun 11CN31	North Node 18TA31	Moon 01GE04
Mercury 20GE07	Venus 25TA56	Mars 29LE45
Jupiter 04GE44	Saturn 26SA07R	Uranus 11AR18
Neptune 29LE22	Pluto 17CN44	

Now you make some decisions. First you know that the planets Jupiter, Saturn, Uranus, Neptune, and Pluto (these are the heavy planets) move so slowly that there is very little change from one day to the next. The north node doesn't change much from day to day either. You can observe this by scanning down the ephemeris page.

So for eyeballing purposes, you will take the reading directly from the ephemeris for the heavy planets and the north node.

Next, you look at the placements for the remaining five fast planets for the following day, July 5. If any of them changed their sign the following day, make a note of it because in a few moments we will need to do some interpolation. You notice that Mars changed to Virgo on July 5; for now just write down Mars 00VI21.

None of the others changed their sign, so you will use their July 4 locations for your eyeballing—except for the Moon because it moves very fast.

So for the Moon (always) and for Mars in this specific chart, we need to interpolate.

Keep in mind that the positions shown for each day are at midnight (the beginning of the day) in Greenwich, England. For eyeballing, we just assume it is midnight at whatever location the birth took place. This, of course, introduces inaccuracy, but after all we are just eyeballing.

Since the birth time is 9:00 am, that is approximately one-third of the way from the beginning of July 4 to the beginning of July 5. I get this by dividing the 24 hours of the day by 9, which is roughly one-third. Remember, we are just approximating.

Looking at the ephemeris, you can see that the Moon moved 14 degrees from July 4 to July 5. So take one-third of 14, which is approximately 5, and add it to the position of the Moon at the beginning of July 4.

Hence, 01GE04 + 5 degrees = 06GE04. This is what you will use for your eyeballed position of the Moon.

Now do the same for Mars as you did for the Moon. Mars moved approximately 36 seconds from July 4 to July 5. One third of 36 is 12, which you will add to the Mars July 4 position.

Hence, 29LE45 + 12 minutes = 29LE57. This is what you will use for your eyeballed position of Mars.

Here is a comparison of your eyeballed planet locations with the computer calculated planet locations:

	Eyeballed	Calculated	Error
Sun	11CN31	12CN05	34 minutes
N. Node	18TA31	18TA30	1 minute
Moon	06GE04	09GE42	3 degrees 38 min.
Mercury	20GE07	20GE42	35 minutes
Venus	25TA56	26TA31	35 minutes
Mars	29LE57	00V106	9 minutes
Jupiter	04GE44	04GE51	7 minutes
Saturn	26SA07R	26SA06R	1 minute
Uranus	11AR18	11AR19	1 minute
Neptune	29LE22	29LE23	1 minute
Pluto	17CN44	17CN45	1 minute

The eyeballing is very close to calculated accuracy in all cases is it not? All the major aspects between the planets are the same as the calculated aspects, so for aspects we can regard eyeballing as being accurate.

The most serious deviations in the above chart are

the Moon being 3 degrees off, which is still a pretty good guess. And Mars actually was in Virgo in the calculated natal chart rather than in Leo. This would cause some inaccuracy when interpreting Mars-in-sign.

The inaccuracies are due to the differences between the location of the birth (Toledo, Ohio in this case) from the ephemeris, which is charted for Greenwich, England.

The reason Greenwich is chosen as the reference point is that Greenwich is located exactly at zero degrees longitude. This makes it easy then to calculate the differences at other longitudes in the world.

The factors that must be compensated for to get an accurate chart are: longitude, latitude, curvature of the earth, and time zone changes. When you get more experience, you will be able to make a reasonably close eyeballing compensation for these factors also, and thus have an even more accurate guess than the one we have just finished compiling.

Except when I am doing a chart for pay, I almost always just do eyeballing because I have learned to be quite accurate at it. For pay, of course, I use the computer and do it absolutely accurately.

So far we have eyeballed the planet placements by sign and degree and aspect.

Now we need to eyeball the ascendant (rising sign) and then set up the houses and place the planets in the houses.

EYEBALLING THE RISING SIGN

You have probably noticed that no two people with the same Sun sign are exactly alike. In fact, some people with a given Sun sign are very little like their Sun sign traits while others seem to be exactly like a textbook picture of their Sun signs. It is a safe bet that you have a number of characteristics that are completely unlike your own Sun sign. One of the major reasons for the differences is in one's rising sign, or ascendant.

Everyone has a rising sign, and it is every bit as important in determining personal characteristics and traits as is the Sun sign.

The rising sign rules the 1st house in everyone's horoscope. The 1st house has domain over the physical body, personality, personal traits, attitude, physical desires, one's outlook on life, etc. There are about forty major personal factors under 1st house domain. It is the most personal of all twelve houses.

The Sun sign establishes the total basic patterning for a person. The rising sign modifies that patterning to form the uniqueness that is you. Of course, there are many other things besides rising sign that enter into the modification of one's Sun sign, but rising sign is the most prominent modifier. If you understand your basic Sun sign characteristics and your basic rising sign characteristics, you will have a nearly complete understanding of self.

Of course, this goes for your understanding of others also. If you have two friends who are Cancers and one is sloppy while the other is a neat-freak, you will understand why by blending their individual rising signs with their Cancer Sun sign.

Blending Sun signs and rising signs is fun, and you learn a lot of astrology that way. Most importantly, you learn a lot about people that way, and that really is what natal astrology is all about.

Blending Sun signs and rising signs is sort of a game, and you only need three things to play this game:

1. A basic knowledge of all twelve zodiac Sun signs. You have already gotten this knowledge earlier in this book, and you can expand on it by getting more detailed books from your library or bookstore.

2. You must know what the rising sign is. Shortly, I will show you a quick and easy way to determine the rising sign.

3. You must know the time of day the birth took place. Often this information is on the birth certificate. Otherwise, ask the mother. Just a close guess will suffice for our purposes here. If the birth time cannot be determined, use 6 am.

To be absolutely certain of rising signs in one hundred percent of the cases, a complete horoscope chart must be done. This is complex, time consuming, and not necessary for the average astrology buff who wants to enjoy astrology without consulting a professional astrologer or casting an absolutely accurate chart.

I have devised a chart, which is shown in figure 8, that gives you a quick look-up method of determining a rising sign. The chart will not be accurate for one hundred percent of the people, but it is accurate for the majority of people born in the United States or in similar latitudes in other countries.

In the chart, I use the conventional two-letter abbreviation for the zodiac signs: AR (Aries); TA (Taurus); GE (Gemini); CN (Cancer); LE (Leo); VI (Virgo); LI (Libra); SC (Scorpio); SA (Sagittarius); CP (Capricorn); AQ (Aquarius); and PI (Pisces).

Sun signs are listed down the chart; rising signs across the top of the chart. The time range listed in the small squares is the time period for a birth. To find a person's rising sign, look down the chart to his/her Sun sign, then read that line across to the proper birth period. The column in which the birth period occurs has the name of the correct rising sign at the top of the column.

For example, suppose your Sun sign is Capricorn and you were born at 6:15 pm. Look down the left column

Rising Signs

Sun Signs	AR	TA	GE	CN	LE	VI	LI	SC	SA	CP	AQ	PI
AR	5 am 7 am	7 am 9 am	9 am 11 am	11 am 1 pm	1 pm 3 pm	3 pm 5 pm	5 pm 7 pm	7 pm 9 pm	9 pm 11 pm	11 pm 1 am	1 am 3 am	3 am 5 am
TA	3 am 5 am	5 am 7 am	7 am 9 am	9 am 11 am	11 am 1 pm	1 pm 3 pm	3 pm 5 pm	5 pm 7 pm	7 pm 9 pm	9 pm 11 pm	11 pm 1 am	1 am 3 am
GE	1 am 3 am	3 am 5 am	5 am 7 am	7 am 9 am	9 am 11 am	11 am 1 pm	1 pm 3 pm	3 pm 5 pm	5 pm 7 pm	7 pm 9 pm	9 pm 11 pm	11 pm 1 am
CN	11 pm 1 am	1 am 3 am	3 am 5 am	5 am 7 am	7 am 9 am	9 am 11 am	11 am 1 pm	1 pm 3 pm	3 pm 5 pm	5 pm 7 pm	7 pm 9 pm	9 pm 11 pm
LE	9 pm 11 pm	11 pm 1 am	1 am 3 am	3 am 5 am	5 am 7 am	7 am 9 am	9 am 11 am	11 am 1 pm	1 pm 3 pm	3 pm 5 pm	5 pm 7 pm	7 pm 9 pm
VI	7 pm 9 pm	9 pm 11 pm	11 pm 1 am	1 am 3 am	3 am 5 am	5 am 7 am	7 am 9 am	9 am 11 am	11 am 1 pm	1 pm 3 pm	3 pm 5 pm	5 pm 7 pm
LI	5 pm 7 pm	7 pm 9 pm	9 pm 11 pm	11 pm 1 am	1 am 3 am	3 am 5 am	5 am 7 am	7 am 9 am	9 am 11 am	11 am 1 pm	1 pm 3 pm	3 pm 5 pm
SC	3 pm 5 pm	5 pm 7 pm	7 pm 9 pm	9 pm 11 pm	11 pm 1 am	1 am 3 am	3 am 5 am	5 am 7 am	7 am 9 am	9 am 11 am	11 am 1 pm	1 pm 3 pm
SA	1 pm 3 pm	3 pm 5 pm	5 pm 7 pm	7 pm 9 pm	9 pm 11 pm	11 pm 1 am	1 am 3 am	3 am 5 am	5 am 7 am	7 am 9 am	9 am 11 am	11 am 1 pm
CP	11 am 1 pm	1 pm 3 pm	3 pm 5 pm	5 pm 7 pm	7 pm 9 pm	9 pm 11 pm	11 pm 1 am	1 am 3 am	3 am 5 am	5 am 7 am	7 am 9 am	9 am 11 am
AQ	9 am 11 am	11 am 1 pm	1 pm 3 pm	3 pm 5 pm	5 pm 7 pm	7 pm 9 pm	9 pm 11 pm	11 pm 1 am	1 am 3 am	3 am 5 am	5 am 7 am	7 am 9 am
PI	7 am 9 am	9 am 11 am	11 am 1 pm	1 pm 3 pm	3 pm 5 pm	5 pm 7 pm	7 pm 9 pm	9 pm 11 pm	11 pm 1 am	1 am 3 am	3 am 5 am	5 am 7 am

Figure 8. Eyeballing the Rising Sign

to CP then read across until you find the time block in which your birth time falls. In this case, that would be the time block labeled 5 pm/7 pm because 6:15 pm falls within that time period. Then read up that 5 pm/7 pm column to see which zodiac sign is at the top; it is CN (Cancer). So Cancer would be the correct rising time in this example.

Time is listed as standard time. For births during daylight savings time, subtract one hour from the birthtime and use that to reference in this chart. For example, if your birthtime is recorded as 7:30 am DST, use 6:30 am when using this chart.

Once you know both the Sun and rising signs for a person, you can easily tell a great deal about that person. All you need to do is study the Sun sign profiles for both signs and blend them together. For instance, suppose your friend has a Cancer Sun sign and a Leo rising sign. Cancer people tend to be timid, reclusive and home loving. Leos are outgoing, show-offs, and interested in playing. A person with this Cancer-Leo blend is likely to be a fun loving home body who likes to retreat into privacy for a while and then break out and be the life of the party sometimes.

First look up your own rising sign and study how it blends uniquely with your Sun sign to make you the person you are.

Then start doing the same thing with family members. Then friends. You will have fun, fascinate your family and friends, and learn about people and astrology in the process.

A final word about using the rising sign chart. You will notice that certain birth times can fall into two different rising sign time periods. For instance, an Aries Sun sign person who is born at 7 am could fall into either an Aries rising sign or a Taurus rising sign. How do you know which is correct?

The rule of thumb for these borderline time periods is: Use the first rising sign if the birthdate is in the first half of the Sun sign period. Use the second rising sign if the birthdate is in the second half of the Sun sign period.

In this example, the person most likely has an Aries rising sign if his/her birthdate falls in the first fifteen days of Aries: that is, from March 21 to April 4. The person is likely to have a Taurus rising sign if the birthdate is in the last fifteen days of Aries; that is, from April 4 to April 19.

There are exceptions to this rule of thumb. The best way to decide is to look at both rising signs and see which really does fit the person in question when you blend each rising sign with the Sun sign. As soon as you do this, it will become immediately obvious which is the correct rising sign.

Every once in a while you meet a person who is exactly like his/her Sun sign. Most likely this person was born about Sunrise (5 am - 7 am period), and has the same Sun and rising sign. These births are commonly called double Aries, double Taurus, double Gemini, etc.

Now you have written down your eyeballed planet positions based on my birth information, and you have learned how to eyeball a rising sign. The only remaining step is to eyeball my rising sign and then create an eyeballed chart with houses and the planets placed in these houses.

MAKING AN EYEBALLED NATAL CHART

Here is where the greatest inaccuracy of eyeballing comes in—creating the houses. There just is not a guaranteed way to eyeball the houses and feel comfortable about their accuracy.

Given my birth information, and using figure 8, determine my rising sign. Go down the left column to Cancer and then across to 9am. Since 9 is a borderline time, either Leo or Virgo, you make a decision. For these borderline cases, recall that I said if the birthdate is in the first half of the Sun sign period, use the first rising sign. If the birth date is in the second half of the Sun sign period, use the second rising sign.

My birth date is July 4, which is in the first half of the Sun sign period. Therefore, you know my rising sign is Leo because Leo comes before Virgo. But what degree of Leo? Here is where you make an educated guess.

Think about it a moment. You know from figure 8 that my 9 am birth time is borderline to Virgo. Therefore guess at a degree that is in the latter degrees of Leo.

Here is a good rule of thumb (still using my example): For 7 am use 1 degree Leo; for 8 am (the halfway point) use 15 degrees Leo; for 9 am use 29 degrees Leo.

Apply this same logic to the other time periods for all your rising sign eyeballing. You will be as close as you can get by eyeballing. With this method, your 1st house cusp will not be in error by more than about 14 degrees, worst case, and usually closer than that.

Now take a blank horoscope chart and label the first house cusp (the rising sign) with 29LE00 (29 degrees 0 seconds of Leo). This then will be the eyeballed rising sign for my birth chart.

To digress a moment. If you do not have a pad of horoscope charts, you can easily make one. Just turn a bowl or plate upside down on a sheet of paper and trace around it. Then you have the circle. Now use a ruler to divide it into twelve pie shaped sections. Don't be overly concerned about making the pie shaped equal sizes. You can label the houses 1 through 12 starting at the 1st house and numbering counterclockwise. Refer to figures 1, 2 or 9 for an idea of the general layout.

Now comes the most inaccurate part of the entire

eyeballing process—setting up houses 2 through 12. There simply is no way to guess accurately. So here is what you do.

You set up all houses to be equal. That is, put 29LE00 on the 1st house cusp, 29VI00 on the 2nd house cusp, 29LI00 on the 3rd and so on through 29CN00 on the 12th house cusp.

Next place the eyeballed planets in the houses. Figure 9 shows what your final eyeballed chart should look like.

Compare figure 9 with the computerized chart, figure 1. Pretty darn close aren't they? There are only two items that do not match closely: (1) the eyeballed Venus falls into the 9th house instead of the 10th where it should be, and (2) Mars is in Leo when it should be in Virgo.

This is phenominally close. Eyeballing does work quite well. If you were to analyze the eyeballed chart, the analysis would be amazingly close to the analysis of the computerized chart.

The principal differences would be these:

1. Mars in Leo would reflect me as being more openly aggressive than I really am with Mars in Virgo. Also, it would show me less skillful with words than I really am with Mars in Virgo.

2. Venus in the 9th house would reflect me being a stronger candidate for a religious life or in the publishing business as perhaps an editor or in marketing rather than as a writer interacting with the public as my Venus in the 10th reflects.

Otherwise the charts would interpret much the same.

The degree of error with eyeballing, if you do it right, is so minimal that it is well worth pursuing. Of course, I do not purport that eyeballing is a replacement for an accurately constructed chart.

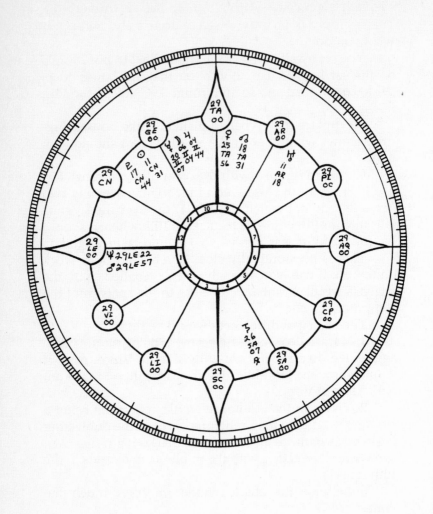

Figure 9
An Eyeballed Natal Chart

The one feature that does not correlate between figures 1 and 9 is that of the houses. None of the eyeballed house cusps have the correct degree on them, and most are not even close. However, they do correlate with regard to the signs ruling the houses.

If you were to eyeball my wife's natal chart (see figure 4) you would not have the signs on the houses correlate because she has two intercepted signs, and there is no way to know that when you are eyeballing. When eyeballing houses, you must assume that it will be a conventional wheel such as in my natal chart.

Eyeballing does come close enough, in general, to matching a calculated chart that you can glean a great deal of valuable information from an eyeballed chart. When you get accustomed to eyeballing, you can set up a chart in a matter of minutes.

In more advanced astrology, the exact degrees on all the house cusps and for all the planets are also analyzed. This gives a deeper and broader scope of interpretation. Analyzing the degrees lets you get deeper inside the person. For this, you must have an accurately constructed chart—no eyeballing.

We will not go into analysis of degrees in this book, but I just want to make you aware that it does exist. In the latter part of this book I will refer you to a good reference book for degree analysis if it should interest you.

10

The Original Way— By Math

Roll up your sleeves, sharpen your pencils, get plenty of paper, and get your calculator if you have one. In this chapter you will learn how to construct an accurate natal chart step by step, doing the calculations yourself, the same way the computer does it.

If you really do not want to learn how to create a natal chart, that is OK. Most of you won't want to, preferring instead computerized charts or eyeballing. In this case, I recommend that you at least read this chapter without actually doing the steps because you will gain an awareness of all the factors involved. In addition, there are some terms used that are not mentioned elsewhere in this book and it would benefit you to at least be familiar with the terms.

Of course, if you want to become a real pro or a top notch amateur, you should definitely take the time to learn the method of chart calculation in this chapter.

The method in this chapter is the one I used for many years in my pre-computer days. It is just as accurate as the computer—just slower—much slower.

I've gained two advantages from knowing how to construct a chart step by step. First, I am able to eyeball a chart faster and more accurately because my mind can approximate the adjustments that must be made. Second, when I make an error in entering data into the computer, or when I read any chart that contains a significant error, it is immediately apparent to me because I know approximately what the chart should look like.

Here are two example of some of the many errors I have encountered.

Case #1: A woman I knew quite well hired me to do her chart and give her an analysis. She gave me her birth information. The moment I glanced at the chart, I knew she had given me incorrect information because the chart was nothing like the person I knew she really was. She insisted, "I copied the information from my birth certificate!" I asked to see the birth certificate. It read 12:05 pm; she had written 12:05 am. Twelve hours difference is tremendous. Even the short time between the birth of identical twins makes a difference.

From Case #1, learn to be careful, detail conscious, and double check everything. Probably 90 percent of the errors I encounter are due to erroneous birth information.

Case #2: A woman, whom I did not know, wrote and asked me to do a chart and analysis and mail it to her. I did a computerized chart.

She replied to tell me that I was a lousy astrologer. Her proof was a photocopy of a hand created chart done "by a world famous astrologer." She mentioned his name, which I promptly forgot because I'd never heard of him.

This hand drawn chart had two significant errors that were apparent at a glance. First, it had Venus trine the Sun, which is absolutely impossible! The Sun and Venus are never separated by more than 48 degrees. Second, it had Pluto in Gemini, which meant she had to have been born sometime prior to May 26, 1914 because that is the last day that Pluto was in Gemini in the past several hundred years. Yet she gave her birthdate as being in 1927.

I wrote to tell her this only to receive a scathing response that I was not competent.

Astrology certainly brings interesting experiences.

Now let's proceed with erecting a natal chart. We will use the ephemeris page shown in figure 3, a Tables of Houses, a logarithm chart (which I will call a "log" chart from now on), a blank horoscope chart, a table of geographical coordinates, and a book of time changes. I will discuss each of these items in sufficient detail for you to use them.

Before we begin the actual calculation, lets examine some of the factors required for the calculation.

Tables of Houses

A Tables of Houses is a book that contains 360 charts, one for each degree of the horoscope wheel. Each chart contains the data necessary to calculate the degrees and signs on each house cusp for a given birth time and place. Figure 10 contains simulations of the two charts required to calculate the house cusps we are going to use in the example we will work in a few moments.

Keep in mind that a complete Tables of Houses has 360 charts, each one different from the others. In figure 10, I have just included enough information to give you an idea of what each table looks approximately like. In an actual Table of Houses book, there would be a listing of all 60 degrees north latitude. I've just included a few of them for illustration.

Most Tables of Houses books contain additional valuable information such as geographical coordinates for major cites of the world and time zone tables.

	3h 12m 0s — 48° 0' 0" — 20 TA 26					LAT.	3h 16m 0s — 49° 0' 0" — 21 TA 26				
	11	12	ASC	2	3		11	12	ASC	2	3
	18GE58	16CN36	15LE32	16VI57	19LI30	0	19GE53	17CN32	16LE33	18VI02	20LI34
	19 37	17 52	16 58	17 16	19 16	5	20 37	18 48	17 57	18 20	20 19
	20 18	19 09	18 20	17 35	19 02	10	21 18	20 04	19 18	18 37	20 05
	20 59	20 27	19 41	17 53	18 48	15	21 55	21 22	20 37	18 53	19 50
	21 43	21 48	21 01	18 11	18 33	20	22 39	22 42	21 55	19 10	19 34
	The table would continue for latitudes 21 through 38						*The table would continue for latitudes 21 through 38*				
	25 15	27 45	26 19	19 25	17 30	39	26 11	28 36	27 07	20 18	18 28
	25 29	28 07	26 37	19 29	17 26	40	26 25	28 58	27 25	20 22	18 24
	25 44	28 30	26 56	19 33	17 22	41	26 40	29 21	27 43	20 26	18 20
	26 00	28 54	27 15	19 38	17 18	42	26 55	29 44	28 01	20 30	18 15
	26 16	29 18	27 34	19 42	17 14	43	27 12	00LE08	28 20	20 34	18 11
	The table would continue for latitudes 44 through 59						*The table would continue for latitudes 44 through 59*				
	03CN50	08LE35	21VI59	21VI17	15LI39	60	04CN43	09LE18	04VI36	22VI01	16LI30

Figure 10. Simulated Placidus Table of Houses
For Latitudes 0° to 60° North

Geographical Coordinates

Geographical coordinates define the exact point on earth where a birth takes place. The coordinates are expressed in degrees and minutes of latitude and longitude. The coordinates are needed whenever you create an accurate natal chart, whether by hand calculation or by computer. The only way a computer knows how to create a chart is for you to key in the geographical coordinates as well as the date and time of birth.

A simulated mini-sample of a typical listing of coordinates found in most tables of houses books is as follows:

Longitudes and Latitudes of Major Cities

Thousand Oaks, CA	118W50	34N10	7:55:20
Titusville, FL	80W49	28N37	5:23:16
Toledo, OH	**83W33**	**41N39**	**5:34:12**
Topeka, KS	95W40	39N03	6:22:40
Torrance, CA	118W19	33N50	7:53:16

The Toledo, Ohio listing above is in bold face because that is the one we will use in the chart we will construct.

The 83W33 indicates 83 degrees and 33 minutes west of zero longitude, which runs through Greenwich, England.

The 4lN39 indicates 41 degrees and 39 minutes north of the equator. The 5:34:12 is longitude time in degrees, minutes and seconds. It can also be written as 5:34' 12," where ' = minutes and " = seconds. Some books do not give the longitude time, so it must be calculated. Figure 11 shows how to calculate longitude time if you should ever need to.

There will be many times when you need to calculate a chart for a birthplace that is not a major city and will not be listed in a convenient table. Villages and rural areas, for example.

Figure 11. Longitude Time

Rule: Each degree of longitude is equal to 4 minutes of clock time.

Longitude for Toledo, Ohio is 83 W 33.

Step 1
$$\begin{array}{r} 83 \text{ degrees} \\ \times \quad 4 \text{ minutes} \\ \hline 332 \text{ minutes} \end{array}$$

Step 2
$$\begin{array}{r} 5 \text{ hours} \\ 60 \overline{)\ 332} \\ \underline{300} \\ 32 \text{ minutes} \end{array}$$

Step 3
$$\begin{array}{r} 33 \text{ minutes} \\ \times \quad 4 \text{ seconds} \\ \hline 132 \text{ seconds} \end{array}$$

(Each minute of longitude must equal 4 seconds of clock time.)

Step 4
$$\begin{array}{r} 2 \text{ minutes} \\ 60 \overline{)\ 132} \\ \underline{120} \\ 12 \text{ seconds} \end{array}$$

Step 5   Add the results of steps 2 and 4 together.

$$\begin{array}{r} 5 \text{ hours} \quad 32 \text{ minutes} \\ + \quad \quad \quad 2 \text{ minutes } 12 \text{ seconds} \\ \hline 5 \text{ hours} \quad 34 \text{ minutes } 12 \text{ seconds} \end{array}$$

This is the total Toledo longitude time.

Compare this result with the listing of coordinates in the Longitudes and Latitudes of Major Cities chart and you will see that they are identical.

In these cases you need to figure out the geographical coordinates using a map (world atlas or road map). Most maps have latitude and longitude marks at intervals around the periphery of the map. These are usually printed in very small letters; I've seen them in black, red, and blue ink. Most commonly they will mark off every four degrees of latitude and longitude. What you need to do is find the birthplace on the map as closely as you can and then interpolate the coordinates using the ones marked on the map as a guide.

This is quite simple. For example, suppose one latitude mark is 34 degrees and the next one is 38 degrees and your birthplace lies three-fourths of the way past 34 toward the 38 degree mark. Use a ruler to measure. The birthplace would be three-fourths of 4 (the distance between marks) past 34. Three-fourths of 4 is 3. So add 3 to 34 and the birthplace is at 37 degrees N latitude. Do the same kind of measurement for the longitude, and then you have the geographical coordinates.

A Tables of Houses is a must for doing hand calculations. You can get one at the library or purchase one. I recommend purchase because they are not expensive and you will use them constantly.

Logarithm Chart

Figure 12 is a log table. It is a mathematical table that is used for hundreds of mathematical calculations, not just for astrology exclusively.

In astrology, the chart is used to calculate the exact position of each planet with respect to the place of birth.

Do not let the impressive appearance of the table intimidate you. It is quite simple to use. You simply look up numbers. Shortly, I will give you a step by step example.

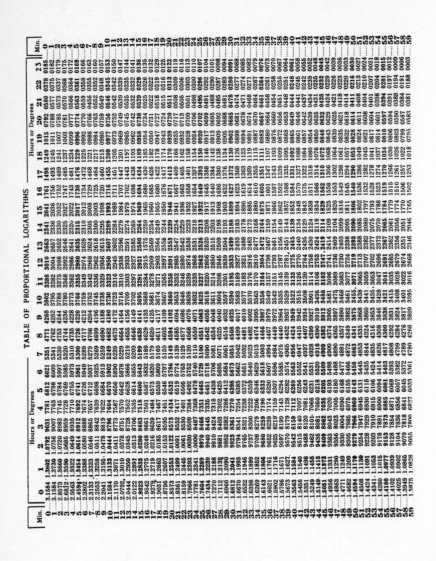

Figure 12
Table of Proportional Logarithms

Time Changes

There are books you can get at the library or purchase that show the various time changes in the United States over the years.

To calculate a natal chart you need to know the time zone and the kind of time in effect at the moment of birth.

For example, Toledo, Ohio is in the Eastern Time Zone, which is known as Zone 5 because it is five time zones west of Greenwich, England.

On July 4, 1929, Toledo was using Eastern Standard Time. However, on July 4, 1990 Toledo was using Eastern Daylight Time, which is one hour faster than standard time.

If all time zones switched uniformly from standard time to daylight time it would be a simple matter to automatically subtract the one hour from daylight time when calculating a chart. However, the switching of times is anything but uniform.

Some places don't switch at all. Some states allow each county to choose whether or not to switch. And then there were War Time changes at various times in various places. It is a mess. The only way to know for certain is to look it up in a book. I've recommended such a book in Part IV of this book.

For our calculations in this chapter, I will tell you the correct time to use.

The Chart

Figure 13 is the chart we will use for the hand calculated natal chart for 9 am, July 4, 1929 at Toledo, Ohio.

I will show you how to calculate the mid-heaven and ascendant cusps and how to calculate the Sun position. All the other house cusps and planet positions are calculated in exactly the same manner, and you can do them or not as you choose. I've filled in those we calculate in this example in the chart.

Name W. W. Hewitt

Birthdate July 4, 1929

Birthplace Toledo, Ohio

Birthtime 9 am EST

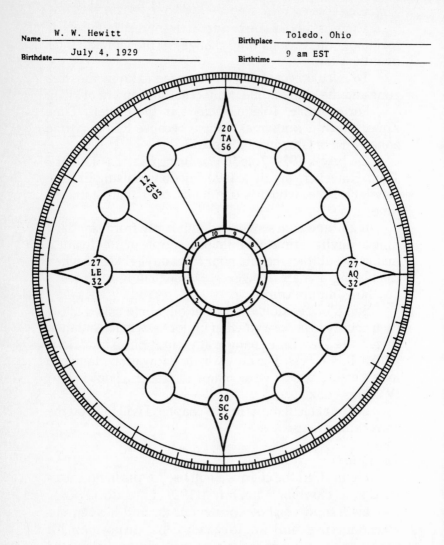

Figure 13
Natal Chart

There are a number of designs of blank charts in pad form available at reasonable prices. The one shown here is just one type. Or you can make your own.

Chart Calculation

In order to determine the house cusps, we first must calculate the "Sidereal Time of Birth." Figure 14 shows step by step how to do this simple calculation. This calculation is to compensate for the time difference and curvature of the earth from Greenwich, England to the point of birth (Toledo, Ohio in this case).

The ephemeris page, figure 3, used for this calculation is a midnight ephemeris. That is, the data given is for zero hours, the very beginning of the day.

Some ephemeris books are noon ephemeris. I've made a note in figure 14 to tell you what you need to do differently if you use a noon ephemeris.

Figure 14 is self-explanatory, so I won't belabor the matter by talking you through it here. The result of our calculation in figure 14 is a sidereal time of 3:14' 12." We will now use this number to look up data in the table of house, figure 10.

In the upper left corner of the lefthand chart in figure 10 you see the numbers 3h 12m 0s. In the same place in the righthand chart you see the numbers 3h 16m 0s. The sidereal time of birth for the example we are working is 3h 14m 12s, which is almost exactly halfway between these two consecutive charts. So to find the house cusps for our natal chart we will have to interpolate halfway between the two table of houses charts in figure 10.

Also take note that running vertically between the two charts is a listing of latitudes (abbreviated LAT.) from 0 to 60 degrees. The birth latitude in our example is 41N39, which is about two-thirds of the way between the 41 and 42 degree latitude figures. Therefore, we will have to interpolate two-thirds of the way between the latitude figures.

Figure 14. Chart Calculation

Birth Date: July 4, 1929; Time: 9:00 am; Place: Toledo, Ohio

Step 1	9:00 am EST	Birth time (less one hour if needed for daylight savings time or War time)
Step 2	+00:00	If pm birth time, add 12:00 hours; add zero for am.

	9:00	
Step 3	+ 5:00	Add time zone hours (see zone chart below) to convert to GMT.

	14:00 GMT	
Step 4	18:46'04"	To GMT, add sidereal time from ephemeris (see fig. 3).

	32:46'04"	
Step 5	5:34'12"	Subtract longitude time (see chart earlier in this chapter). (For subtraction, this is the same as 32:45'64".)

	27:11'52"	See GMT correction chart below for further instruction
Step 6	2'20"	Add correction for GMT (see chart below).

	27:13'72"	If this number is more than 24:00:00, subtract 24:00:00 from it.
	24:00:00	

	3:13'72"	= **3:14'12"**, which is the sidereal time of birth.

FOR NOON EPHEMERIS: The rules are slightly different if you are using a noon ephemeris (the above calculations are for a midnight ephemeris). In constructing a chart using a noon ephemeris, Step 2 above is exactly opposite. That is, in Step 2 add 12:00 hours for an am birth time, and add 00:00 for a pm birth time. All other calculations are as shown above.

Figure 14, Continued

GMT Correction Table

Add 10″ correction for every GMT hour at the end of Step 5. If the number at the end of Step 5 is greater than 24:00:00, subtract 24:00:00 before calculating the GMT correction from the chart below.

0′	to	6′ = 01″		30′	to	36′ = 06″
6′	to	12′ = 02″		36′	to	42′ = 07″
12′	to	18′ = 03″		42′	to	49′ = 08″
18′	to	24′ = 04″		48′	to	54′ = 09″
24′	to	30′ = 05″		54′	to	60′ = 10″

Time Zones

+ 5	for Eastern Standard Time	(EST)
+ 6	for Central Standard Time	(CST)
+ 7	for Mountain Standard Time	(MST)
+ 8	for Pacific Standard Time	(PST)
+10	for Central Alaska Time	(CAT)
+10.5	for Hawaiian Standard Time	(HST)

Centered near the top of the left hand chart you will find 20 TA 26 and in the same place in the righthand chart you will find 21 TA 26. These are the positions for the midheaven (10th house cusp). To find the midheaven for our example chart, we will need to interpolate between these two midheaven positions.

Let's do the midheaven first. The midheaven difference between the two charts is exactly 60 minutes (one degree). Half of 60 is 30. So add 30 minutes to the midheaven position in the lefthand chart and you have 20 TA 26 + 30′ = 20 TA 56, which is the 10th house cusp for our example. Write this on your blank chart as I have done in figure 13.

Since you now know the 10th house cusp, you automatically know the 4th house cusp. It will be the same degree and minutes in the opposite sign, or 20 SC 56. Write this on your chart also.

Now let's do the Ascendant (ASC), or 1st house cusp. The left chart at 41 degrees latitude shows 26 LE 56, and the right chart shows 27 LE 43. They are 47 minutes apart. Half of 47 is 24 (rounded), so add 24 to the lower number: 26 LE 56 + 24 = 27 LE 20.

Do the same type of calculation now for the 42 degree latitude. The left chart shows 27 LE 15 and the right chart shows 28 LE 01. They are 46 minutes apart. Half of 46 is 23 minutes. Add 23 minutes: 27 LE 15 + 23 = 27 LE 38.

Since our birth latitude (41N39) falls 2/3 of the way between the 41st and 42nd degree latitudes, we must now interpolate between the numbers we calculated in the two previous paragraphs.

The difference between 27 LE 38 and 27 LE 20 is 18 minutes. Two-thirds of 18 is 12. Add 12: 27 LE 20 + 12 = 27 LE 32, which is the degree and sign of our calculated Ascendant. Enter this on the 1st house cusp of your chart. Of course, this automatically makes the 7th house cusp become 27 AQ 32; enter this on your chart also.

When you compare our calculations so far against the computer generated ones (see figure 1) you will see a minute or so difference. The reason is that I have used rounded minutes and no seconds in my ephemeris page, table of houses page, and my calculations for simplicity. The computer uses minutes and seconds and fractions of seconds and does no rounding until the final calculation. The rounded calculations I use are certainly close enough, and for all practical purposes can be considered precise. When I first started in astrology, I used seconds and fractions of seconds just like the computer, but found it to be too cumbersome for general use.

If you choose you can proceed to calculate the remaining house cusps in the same manner as I've just explained. If they vary significantly from the computer generated figures, recheck your math.

Figure 15 is self-explanatory and shows step by step how to calculate planet positions. The Sun is used as an example and is filled in on figure 13. If you choose you can calculate the remaining planets and fill them in on your chart.

You now have been introduced to the three methods of creating a natal chart: By computer, by eyeballing, and by hand calculated math. Whichever method you choose is up to you. Interpreting the results is the same for all three methods, and you will learn how to do interpretations in the next several chapters.

Figure 15. Planet Correction

With a midnight ephemeris, always use the Greenwich day of birth and the day following when finding the movement of a planet in a 24-hour period. The same applies to using a noon ephemeris, with the following exception: For am births where the GMT is less than 24:00, use the previous day and the birth day.

The planet positions are given in the ephemeris (figure 3 for our purposes here).

First you must determine the constant log from the log chart in figure 12 that represents the GMT of the birth time. The GMT is the number you obtained at the completion of Step 3 in figure 14 when calculating the chart. In our example case, the GMT is 14:00. In cases where the GMT is 24:00 or more, subtract 24 to obtain the GMT number to use here.

Now look up 14 degrees and 00 minutes in the log chart in figure 12. Go across the top to 14 and down to 0. The number is .2341. So the constant log for this specific birth is .2341. It is usually written CL .2341. This same constant log will be used to calculate all of the planet positions for this specific birth.

Sun position at midnight Greenwich on July 4, 1929 is: 11 CN 32

Sun position at midnight Greenwich on July 5, 1929 is: 12 CN 29

To find the movement of the Sun in this 24 hour period, subtract 11 CN 32 from 12 CN 29.

$$\begin{aligned} 12 \text{ CN } 29 &= 11 \text{ CN } 89 \\ -11 \text{ CN } 32 &= \underline{11 \text{ CN } 32} \\ &\quad\ 00 \qquad 57' \text{ movement} \end{aligned}$$

Now refer to the log chart in figure 12 to find the log equivilent of 57'. Look down to left column to 57 and then over to 0 (because there are zero degrees). You find the number 1.4025.

Figure 15, Continued

Add the constant log to the Sun log number:

Sun 1.4025
CL .2341
1.6366

Now look up 1.6366 in the log chart to see what degrees and minutes comes closest to it. You will find that 00 degrees and 33 minutes comes closest to 1.6366. This means that the Sun moved 33' from the position listed in the ephemeris until the birth time and place being charted. To find where the Sun was at 9 am on July 4, 1929 in relation to Toledo, Ohio, add the 33' to the ephemeris position:

Ephemeris 11 CN 32
Movement 00   33
Position   11 CN 65 = 12 CN 05

If you look at the computer calculated position for the Sun in figure 1, you will see it exactly matches the position calculated above.

All planet positions are calculated exactly as described above. The only things different will be the ephemeris numbers and the constant log because the birth times and places will be different for each chart you construct.

PART III

INTERPRETING
A
NATAL CHART

11

Planets in the Signs

This chapter and the three following chapters are designed to give you a quick reference for interpreting the various factors that go into compiling a complete natal horoscope interpretation.

For example, if a chart has Mercury in Gemini, look up the brief interpretation for it in this chapter. Combine it with all the other pertinent interpretations and you end up with a good overall interpretation for the chart.

The interpretations in these four chapters are brief, covering only some of the salient points. For more depth and details, you will need to read more extensive books that specialize just in interpretations. These chapters do, however, provide accurate and sufficiently complete information for beginners to get an excellent start on their path to the enjoyment and practice of astrology.

SUN

The Sun in the Signs

An entire chapter, Chapter 4, was devoted to Sun signs because the Sun is the single most important planet in any chart. The Sun will not be covered additionally here except to point out that in any chart the Sun represents the self—body and personality. Colors associated with the Sun are gold and orange. Refer to Chapter 4 for details.

MOON

Moon in Aries

Gives a person a great deal of energy. Confers ambition. Inclines person to temper flare–ups and impetuousness. Person is usually courageous and confident. These people do not tolerate interference from others. They are independent and do what they want, right or wrong. There usually is a capacity for leadership.

Moon in Taurus

These people tend to have steady emotions. On the positive side, these people are hard working, patient, and appreciate the fine things in life. Negatively, they are lazy, very stubborn, materialistic, and unwilling to change. These people are good at handling money and domestic matters. They often attract the good things in life. Often they have a green thumb.

Moon in Gemini

This confers quick–wit, ability to communicate both in writing and speaking. Negatively, these people can be unreliable and untrustworthy. Positively, they are intelligent, versatile, ingenious, and adaptable. Sometimes they talk too much. If the Moon is heavily afflicted with harsh aspects (squares, oppositions), it indicates much confusion and distorted reasoning. If the Moon has favorable aspects (trines, sextiles, or conjunctions), it indicates persons who have excellent ability to think and rationalize clearly and who are resourceful.

Moon in Cancer

The Moon is most powerful here. On the positive side, they are warm, loving, maternal, romantic. On the negative side, they are overly romantic, have a smothering affection, like to hoard things, and often have a mean streak. Domestic security is vitally important to these people, and they can have strong ties to their mother. These people are usually good cooks. They often are overly sensitive to the remarks and actions of others, which can cause them to withdraw and brood.

Moon in Leo

These people want to be the center of attention. Often they are prima donnas. They need recognition – to be admired and appreciated. They are capable of great love and great ambition. Negatively, they can be egotistical show-offs. Positively, they are enthusiastic, responsible, devoted, kind, and generous. These people have a tendency to dominate others. They love children, but expect them to be well groomed.

Moon in Virgo

These people are hardworking, pay great attention to detail, and are very fussy about cleanliness and good nutrition. If well aspected, it confers cleverness and ingenuity. If harshly aspected it usually confers slyness, nagging, and perhaps a touch of greed. Most often these people are shy and prefer to work behind the scenes, avoiding the limelight.

Moon in Libra

Strong sensitivity to others, especially marriage and business partners. With good aspects, these people are balanced, humble, courteous, and gentle. With adverse aspects, these people are unbalanced and do nearly everything in extremes. These people often are well suited for public relations work. Their link to their parents, and especially the mother, is quite strong.

Moon in Scorpio

This is not a favorable position for the Moon. These people are strong headed and biased to the extreme. Positively, they can be quite passionate and have ample self–confidence; they can be psychic and have compassion for others. Negatively, they can be cruel, rude, stubborn, and selfish.

Moon in Sagittarius

These are optimistic, cheerful people who love the outdoors and foreign travel. They tend to be idealistic, often overly idealistic. They usually follow traditional religious and philosophical views. If adversely aspected, they can be nervous, restless, and discontented most of the time. With positive aspects, they are little rays of sunshine in everyone's life.

Moon in Capricorn

These people are usually ambitious, hard workers whose main goal is personal financial security. They are much more materialistic than spiritual. Everything they do is with self–interest in mind. With positive aspects, they can be witty and faithful. With negative aspects, they can be unscrupulous.

Moon in Aquarius

Indicates dealing with the public. These are the friendly humanitarians who somehow manage to remain impersonal while being the champion of human causes. They can be quite stubborn. Often they have strong psychic abilities. Freedom is all important to these people.

Moon in Pisces

This is an exceptionally strong psychic position. These people are very sensitive and emotional. This Moon position is often associated with outstanding artistic, musical, or poetic ability. Because of their sensitivity, these people become easily hurt by the words and actions of others. Sometimes they become neurotic or psychotic. Sometimes they are extremely timid.

MERCURY

Mercury in Aries

A quick, alert mind. Sometimes jumps impetuously to conclusions without giving the matter sufficient thought. There can sometimes be a quick temper or irritability. These people are decisive and competitive. They make decisions based more on a personal point of view rather than on impersonal facts. They have good minds, but sometimes become egotistical, sarcastic, and changeable.

Mercury in Taurus

These people appreciate beauty. Their thought processes are geared toward what is practical, material, or financially beneficial. These are not necessarily brilliant thinkers, nor are they usually original, but they are shrewd in business. They often make good managers. In extreme cases, there can be dullness or lust.

Mercury in Gemini

Mercury is most powerful here. These are the very bright people who can write and speak well. Professional communicators often have this placement in their natal chart. It is nearly impossible to out think these people; they have exceptionally agile minds. If harshly aspected, it can cause acute nervousness, often to the point of mental burnout. If these people lack self–discipline they will become a jack of all trades and a master of none. These people need to guard against allowing themselves to become sidetracked from their main goal.

Mercury in Cancer

Love of history and antiques is indicated here. Much of their thinking concerns their home and domestic matters. In business, they are most suited for real estate, food, and consumer products. Adverse aspects to this position often confers cruelty.

Mercury in Leo

Unique capacity for leadership on the positive side. Self–centered and domineering on the negative side. These people have strong willpower and usually a one–track mind focused on what it is they want. Great self–confidence goes with this placement, also. These people are slow to make up their minds, and equally slow to change their minds. Their special areas of interest are the stock market, theater, investments, artistic pursuits, and education. They like to combine travel to be both work and pleasure.

Mercury in Virgo

Mercury is very strong here. These people are detail conscious to the extreme. They make good researchers. Their minds are analytical, and they have great reasoning ability. They insist on precision and orderliness. They are efficient. These people do best when they have a specialized skill or are well educated. These people are work oriented and do not waste time. Any work requiring exactness is for them. Some suitable occupational areas are mathematics, medicine, and hygiene.

Mercury in Libra

Positively, these people are balanced and have vision. Negatively, they are unbalanced and lack vision. Some good fields for these people are astrology, public relations, psychology, counseling, and law. These people have hardworking, stern minds and expect others to be the same way. They are repulsed by bad manners.

Mercury in Scorpio

Positively, these people are spiritual, wise, and seek great depths of understanding. Negatively, they are self–centered and concerned only with gratifying their physical desires. This position confers an intuitive mind capable of great insights. When they speak, they say exactly what they think regardless of how it affects others. Very determined minds are indicated here that can, in extreme cases, become scheming minds. These people make good investigators and researchers. If Mercury is heavily afflicted with harsh aspects, then there can be excessive preoccupation with sex.

Mercury in Sagittarius

The mind is concerned with social justice, law, religion, philosophy, and higher education. This is not the best placement for Mercury, often causing the persons to lose sight of truth. These people frequently have the gift of prophecy. These people sometimes become so concerned about conformity that they become hypocrites. They often consider themselves to be authorities (know it all). They need to realize that just because a current trend is popular, it does not necessarily mean it is right.

Mercury in Capricorn

Ambition and visionary are the key words here. Also shrewd, practical, and status conscious. These are realistic people. In extreme cases, they will do whatever it takes to get what they want without regard to right or wrong. Generally, however, they work hard to get the education they need to succeed, and they do succeed without resorting to anything underhanded. These people do not waste their time with theories or lofty thoughts—they think the only ideas that are good are those that have some practical value.

Mercury in Aquarius

These are big thinkers, large scale thoughts, often concerned with masses of people (the public). No time wasted here on small or petty thinking. These are usually open minded people who seek truth. Mercury is strong here and often confers a highly evolved mind—intuitive, or concerned with the betterment of humanity. This is an excellent position for astrologers or for occult disciplines in general. These people seek mental stimulation through friends and groups of people.

Mercury in Pisces

These people usually have photographic memories and vivid imaginations. They are highly intuitive and telepathic. These are sympathetic people who are often too easily swayed by others. Negatively, they can be weak willed or wallow in self-pity. If Mercury is adversely aspected, it often indicates a persecution complex.

VENUS

Venus in Aries

These people demand personal attention and tend to be self–centered. They pursue their love interest with vigor. In a woman's chart, it indicates a woman who is usually the aggressor (chases the man). Sometimes these people are bullies.

Venus in Taurus

Venus is very strong here, both for good and for bad. On the up side, these are loving, compassionate people. On the down side, these are brutish, gluttonous people. In any case, these people are always intense in their pursuits. These people love comfort, luxury, beauty, and the good life in general. They almost always keep their homes beautiful, often with artsy objects. Talented singers often have this placement of Venus in their natal chart.

Venus in Gemini

These people often marry more than once because they need more than one outlet for their affection. It is not uncommon for them to have twins. Variety in love life, variety in travel, variety in all emotional pursuits are the key phrases for this Venus. These people really are offended by crude behavior. Often they are superficial in their professed romantic interests.

Venus in Cancer

Mother instinct. Self–sacrificing. Also can be changeable and selfish. Deeply sensitive about their romantic feelings. They assume a dignified facade to cover their easily hurt feelings. They can be moody and unpredictable, which can be threatening to a successful marriage. Women with this position are very domestic; they love to cook and keep house. Men with this position often "mother" their families.

Venus in Leo

These people love drama. Their personal behavior is dramatic, they are born romantics and they like their romances to be dramatic and exciting. They dramatize their emotions, like to be the center of attention. These are very social people. They love to throw parties, the more lavish, the better. They are warm, outgoing, and affectionate. They are loyal to those people they think are worthy of their loyalty. Sometimes these people are prima donnas, and at social gatherings make a concerted effort to vie for attention. They love children. In some cases, these people become possessive and jealous. They are usually excellent actors and actresses.

Venus in Virgo

This is not the best position for Venus. Usually one of two extremes characterize this position. (1) Vicious, sly, underhanded, overly critical of others (never of self), difficult to get along with, crude, sloppy, promiscuous. (2) Humble, shy, self–sacrificing to help others, neatness freaks, well mannered, clean, extremely faithful, nurturing. Often they are a mixture of some of each of these two extremes. Probably there are more unmarried people with this Venus placement than any other. These people often make good doctors and nurses, cooks, dietitians.

Venus in Libra

This is a powerful position for Venus. It bestows general personal physical attractiveness and attractiveness to the opposite sex. Marriage is important to these people and they generally have many opportunities for marriage. They have a strong sense of justice. These people are easy to get along with. They are refined and have an innate understanding of other people. Women with this position desire to be deeply cared for, and they want their men to be well poised and suave in public. This is a good position for success in the performing arts.

Venus in Scorpio

Sex is the keyword here. Strong emotions and sexual desires. Passionate, jealous, secretive, and sensual. Positively, these people are faithful and enduring. Negatively, lustful and demanding. Under all circumstances these people maintain their dignity and pride. Women with this placement sometimes use their sex appeal to gain power and to manipulate people. Love–hate relationships are common, and once a romance is broken or turns cold, it is never mended.

Venus in Sagittarius

You never feel neutral about these people. You either love them or detest them because of their potential extremes of behavior (or a mixture thereof). For examples, they can be open, honest, forthright, unafraid, religious, moral; or they can be blunt to the point of offensiveness, impractical, cruel, self–centered, do things only for selfish purposes, try to impose their religious beliefs on others.

Usually these people like outdoor sports, are fond of horses, and often seek to marry people of foreign extraction or even other races. They also prefer people with higher education.

Venus in Capricorn

Ambitious, calculating, dependable. They often seek a marriage partner who will increase their station (status) in life. They show their emotion in their actions rather than in words. They are proud and reserved and are often perceived as being snobbish. In public they suppress their emotions and sexuality, but can be quite demonstrative in private. If they marry young, they quite often seek an older, mature partner. Conversely, if they marry when they are older, they often seek a much younger partner. They are loyal to those they love. Sometimes these people choose careers as antique dealers or work in art galleries and museums. In extreme cases, they are overly concerned about money or status to the exclusion of everything else.

Venus in Aquarius

Impersonal but friendly people. These people are usually well liked because they sparkle with energy, are electric, and have an unusual manner about them. Often they are self–sacrificing to help others. Frequently their romances are sudden and superficial, rather than stable or long lasting. They do not like partners who shy away from social gatherings or events because these are very social, group oriented people. In some cases, these people are eccentric or promiscuous. Any occupation in which electricity or electronics is a major factor is often chosen by these people for their career.

Venus in Pisces

Powerful placement for Venus. Love is at its highest vibration here. Deep compassion, sympathy, and understanding of love and life. These are romantic, sensitive people, and they feel lonely and disappointed if they do not receive demonstrations of love and affection from others. Sometimes their disappointments lead to mental illness or neurosis. This position of Venus probably bestows more innate ability in artistic creativity than any other placement. Many great artists, poets, and composers have Venus in Pisces in their natal charts. Because of their sensitivity, others frequently take advantage of them. They suffer (martyr complex) in silence (usually). In extreme cases, they may lack discrimination, be lazy, or overly dependent on others.

MARS

Mars in Aries

Don't mess with these people. They don't take "nothin' from nobody, no time!" Powerful Mars in Aries bestows courage, great energy, a strong sense of competitiveness, the desire to always win and always be first. They ask no quarter and give none. They have much initiative, are usually headstrong, impulsive, and independent. They love physical games. Football and car racing often appeal to them. These people are never spectators in life—they are full time active participants. Sometimes they have violent tempers, are overly aggressive, or are egotistical. They need to learn to be more patient and loving.

Mars in Taurus

These people are slow, but they have great perseverance and determination. They never give up. They are not aggressive, but if forced to fight they will do so unrelentingly, to the death if necessary. Often their choice of career is in some field that requires patience and persistence such as using tools to create objects that are durable and attractive. They have strong desires for money and possessions and will sometimes gravitate to a career in the money fields such as banking. Men with this Mars placement often lose their hair prematurely.

Mars in Gemini

These people have active, critical minds and often have mechanical or engineering skills. They love to argue and often become irritable. They have good ideas but not necessarily the perseverance to see their ideas through to fruition. This is a common Mars position for news reporters and critics. It is quite likely these people will have many changes of occupation and may even pursue two jobs at the same time.

Mars in Cancer

This is not Mars best position. Often there is moodiness, frustration that leads to anger, intense emotions, lack of harmony on the domestic scene. Suppressed anger can result in ulcers or psychological problems. It can indicate poor relationship with the parents. People with this placement are frequently home improvement buffs, which becomes an outlet for their pent-up frustrations. Occasionally these people have great sympathy for those less fortunate and do work on their behalf.

Mars in Leo

A great deal of willpower, creativity, and energy are associated with this placement. Usually there is much self–confidence and leadership ability. These people must be the center of whatever is going on; they demand attention. Frequently they are egotistical and are show-offs. They are strongly opinionated, and often make enemies because of it. There are only two ways: their way and the wrong way. They have strong attraction to the opposite sex. The men are masculine and proud, but they do tend to lose their hair at a young age. In extreme cases, they can be brassy and unpleasant to be around for very long. Sometimes they are domineering, and believe they are infallible.

Mars in Virgo

This is the sign of the perfectionist. These people are very skillful in their work. They are precise and like to be recognized for their attention to detail. Some occupations associated with this placement are precision machinists, craftsmen, surgeons, nurses, those in the health care profession in general. Sometimes these people are highly critical of others, especially others who are not as detail conscious as they are. People with this placement are methodical and do not take actions unless there is a practical reason to do so. In extreme cases, they get so wrapped up in details that they never see the big picture and do not achieve much at all—the "can't see the forest for the trees" syndrome.

Mars in Libra

These are the social movers and shakers. They direct their immense energy toward social activities of all sorts from social reform to fraternal type activities. These people do not act alone; they must have partners or a group. Social injustice infuriates them, and they will become involved even on issues that do not affect them personally. They desire marriage as an outlet for their own gratification, and seek partners who are aggressive and energetic. While these people are usually aggressive and selfish, they tone it down with social refinement and grace, which makes them more pleasant to be around.

Mars in Scorpio

These people are intense in everything they do. They are uncompromising. Everything they pursue is to the extreme. They either have devoted friends or bitter enemies. They either are devotedly spiritual or have gutter level lust. Nothing is halfway with them. In extreme cases they are full of anger and hold grudges forever. If they are your friend, they will die for you. If you are their enemy, they will stop at nothing to get more than even with you. As employees, they are usually reliable and serious. They have no fear of death. Nothing will deter them from achieving their goals. Exactly how these traits will appear in individual horoscopes depends on the aspects to Mars in that chart. In general, squares from Saturn, Uranus, Pluto or Neptune tend to bring out the worst; the more exact the square, the stronger the influence. The entire chart really needs to be studied to come up with an accurate pronouncement.

Mars in Sagittarius

These people are almost always open and direct in their dealings with others. They play fair, but do interpret the rules to their own advantage. Their motivations are almost always idealistic. They support causes and try to improve their social order. There is a strong love of sports and of hunting. Usually they have strong religious or philosophical beliefs, and in extreme cases try to convert others to their way of thinking. They are reliable, demanding, quick, and are go–getters.

Mars in Capricorn

These people are extremely materialistic and will expend great amounts of energy in their work to achieve status, money, and power so they can satisfy their materialistic craving. They are practical people who know how to use their energies efficiently. Many executives, politicians, and military leaders have this position of Mars in their natal charts. Usually they have good self–discipline. They are able to take and carry out orders from their superiors, and they are also capable of giving orders. They demand obedience and discipline from those under their command. They take great pride in doing their job well, and have no tolerance for laziness. Parents with this placement expect great things from their children and are very disappointed if their children let them down. If Mars is afflicted (has harsh aspects) then there is total disregard for the rights of others—they become selfish, cold, and will run rough shod over anyone in their way.

Mars in Aquarius

These people are happy only when they are dealing with the public in some way. They may be social or anti–social (depending on aspects), but they must interact with masses of people. They desire independence and often follow unorthodox methods. They usually do not work well under authoritarian rules—they want to make their own rules to suit themselves. Negatively, these are the people who try to overthrow the existing social structure or government, often destroying the old ways before they have anything worthwhile to replace the old ways with. Positively, these are the people who seek social justice for all, who will not tolerate prejudice, and who perform social services to help those less fortunate.

Mars in Pisces

These are self–sacrificing people who are more interested in helping others than in their own welfare. They make excellent nurses. Unfortunately, they are easily misused by others who take advantage of their generosity and goodwill. Often these people are considered to be weak because they rarely stand up for their rights. This position favors those who work behind the scenes rather than in public view. This is a favorable position for artistic and musical careers.

JUPITER

Jupiter in Aries

These people are almost always endowed with exceptionally good health and are outgoing, generous, and quite aggressive. If Jupiter is harshly afflicted, then they can become rude and overbearing. They are willing to embark on a large project and pursue it much further than others would be willing to do. Sometimes they become overzealous and pursue a matter to the annoyance of others. These people often become leaders in educational and spiritual matters.

Jupiter in Taurus

These people usually know how to use money and material possessions in a beneficial manner. They also have the tendency to attract money and material goods to themselves. They often find their careers in the world of commerce and business. They love good food and often become overweight. At times they can be jealous and demanding. In extreme cases, they are greedy and suspicious. This is a good placement for those interested in musical or artistic careers. This is also a good position for gardeners.

Jupiter in Gemini

These are brilliant intellectuals who are very adaptable and expressive. However, unless other factors in the natal chart confer self–discipline, these people scatter their mental energies without achieving much. In other words, they can have a broad but superficial knowledge that is not of much worth in dollars and cents. Positively, these people can be skillful writers, educators, lecturers, and leaders who can contribute much to society. Usually there is much traveling in their lives, both mentally and physically, and almost always some foreign travel. Additional vocations are businesses concerned with publishing, travel, importing/exporting, communications, mail–order, and personal services.

Jupiter in Cancer

This is a powerful position for Jupiter. It indicates a good family background—not necessarily wealthy—but rather love, kindness and positive parental influence. Quite often these people become financially well off at some point in their lives. These people are fond of food and are good cooks, often overeating to the point of creating digestive problems. Some careers: real estate, farming, housing, anything in the food industry, articles for use in the home. Sometimes these people have dreams that are not practical. In extreme cases they may be miserly and fickle.

Jupiter in Leo

These people love to do things on a grand scale. They love parades, rituals, drama, fraternal organizations. They are usually quite generous, self–confident, and optimistic. They enjoy giving, but expect to be admired for it. Leadership ability and dignity go with this position. These people have to watch themselves lest they become conceited, arrogant, and overbearing. They love children and are interested in their welfare. Hence, they often become school teachers, Sunday school teachers, scout leaders, etc. They often have a gambling streak in them, including interest in the stock market. Usually an abundance of talent go with this position. If Jupiter is heavily afflicted with harsh aspects, it forewarns of disappointments and losses in love, children, speculation, and romances.

Jupiter in Virgo

This is not the best position for Jupiter. It foretells of overwork. Because they are extremely detail conscious and because they put their entire being into their work, they are in danger of becoming workaholics and burning themselves out. These people are compassionate and will give their all for others. In extreme cases, these people can become tyrants. Usually they have moral integrity. Often these people seek to work in hospitals or educational institutions. If they are wealthy, they usually donate large amounts of money to educational or health causes.

Jupiter in Libra

This confers an enduring marriage and a good home life unless Jupiter is heavily afflicted with harsh aspects. These people usually are well balanced mentally and physically, have good judgment, and much talent. If Jupiter is very heavily afflicted, then there is danger of lawsuits and other legal problems.

Jupiter in Scorpio

These people are often involved on a large scale in matters of corporate finances, insurance, taxes, legacies, death, of real estate. Often they are interested in occult matters, especially in life after death and mental telepathy. They can be intense and uncompromising in their beliefs, thus creating many enemies. If Jupiter is well aspected to Uranus, Neptune or Pluto, these people can be quite gifted psychically. If harshly aspected to these planets, then there is usually unwise or illegal use of psychic ability such as manipulating others for personal gain.

Jupiter in Sagittarius

Jupiter is powerful here. Positively, it indicates people who are straightforward, generous, deep thinkers, and farsighted. They are interested in foreign cultures, education, philosophy, and religion. Negatively, it indicates narrowmindedness, demanding, and even vicious.

Jupiter in Capricorn

These people make their own opportunities rather than wait for opportunity. They are conscientious and are willing to work harder than asked. Generally they have moral integrity in business. They tend to have conservative views, and exercise great caution and mature judgment in everything they do. They do have a strong desire for power and status, which often causes problems with their domestic life. This position is typical of the executive who lives at the office and hardly ever sees his family. These people do not like waste and in extreme cases become miserly.

Jupiter in Aquarius

Great tolerance is foretold by this Jupiter position. They do not harbor prejudice and insist on equality in every respect for all people. Positively, these people are statesmanlike and conscientious. Negatively, they are scheming and egocentric. If this Jupiter is well aspected, there can be interest in occult matters, astrology, reincarnation, cosmic law, and humanitarian causes.

Jupiter in Pisces

If this Jupiter has aspects to Uranus, Neptune or Pluto there will most likely be considerable psychic ability and great intuition. These people are extremely compassionate and understanding. In extreme cases, these people can be weak and selfish.

SATURN

Saturn in Aries

This is not the best position for Saturn. People born with this in their natal chart may have to work very hard all their life with very little gain to show for it. These people can be forceful, direct, and domineering. This position also indicates resourcefulness. In highly developed people such as Albert Einstein, who had this placement, it can lead to mental creativity. Sometimes these people can be defensive and difficult to communicate with. In extreme cases, these people can be tyrants.

Saturn in Taurus

If Saturn is well aspected, these people are patient and steady and have practical management ability, especially in areas of finance. They are builders who can acquire much if they are willing to work hard—they get nothing for free. They tend to be frugal. At about age 29 these people seek a career that will provide them with financial and domestic security. Some professions they are especially adept for are: banking, investments, insurance, or business management in general. If Saturn is not well aspected, they can be stubborn, greedy, and miserly.

Saturn in Gemini

Quick mind and quick hands are indicated here. They have well–disciplined, logical minds and are good at problem solving. They are generally adept at mathematics and science and often follow occupations involved with these. They are thorough and well organized and insist on clear communications. As a result, they usually achieve something worthwhile for their efforts. Some additional occupations these people frequently pursue are bookkeepers, secretaries, accountants, writers, researchers, and teachers. They often pursue two jobs at the same time. If Saturn is heavily aspected with harsh aspects, the person will likely be underhanded or prefer stealing or gambling instead of honest work.

Saturn in Cancer

This is not the best position for Saturn. It often indicates a childhood that was cold, unloving, full of problems that leave emotional scars. Nevertheless, these people take their home life seriously and work hard to have a home, even though it may cost them heavy indebtedness. They prefer to work alone and like to work around the home. For all their efforts, they often times never really have a satisfactory home life. On rare occasion, one of these people will be dishonest or lazy.

Saturn in Leo

Hard workers but they don't like to get their hands dirty if they can avoid it. These people have an insatiable need for recognition and for feeling important. Many become actors or other professions where there is a great deal of publicity and public notice. As parents, they are strict disciplinarians. Physically, they are often prone to heart trouble. In addition to all fields of entertainment, they also like speculative investments. If Saturn is heavily afflicted, there can be losses or disappointments with finances or through children.

Saturn in Virgo

Some keywords here are: practical, hard working, precise, perfectionist, detail conscious, accuracy, efficiency, neat, patient. These people typically do not take breaks—they work, work, work, and drive others just as hard. They live by rules, which makes it difficult for others to get along with them at times. They often work in medicine, health or science research, bookkeeping or other record keeping. Often these people become gloomy and austere. They need to develop a sense of humor. Worry and overwork often lead to health problems.

Saturn in Libra

These people often marry late in life or else marry a serious person. The marriage often involves hard work and burdens. This is a powerful position for Saturn and frequently indicates attainment of great wealth and high honors. Lawyers, judges, arbitrators often have this Saturn placement. These people are reliable and humanitarian. Saturn, when afflicted, in all signs tends to produce some sort of criminal behavior. However, in Libra, it tends to produce fewer or less serious criminal activity.

Saturn in Scorpio

There is a strong desire to have authority and a hard drive to attain their ambitions. Whether they use honest, fair methods or underhanded, dishonest methods depends on Saturn's aspects. They can be hard taskmasters. They are fanatical about their principles. They tend to gravitate toward businesses dealing with finances, taxes, insurance, matters concerning property of others. Being a tax accountant in a corporation is an example.

Saturn in Sagittarius

These people have deep concern over their personal reputation. They generally are intelligent and also have self–discipline. If Saturn is well aspected, they make good leaders who are humane and warm. If poorly aspected, they can be dictatorial, demanding, and slave drivers. They like to be regarded as an authority in some way, often in religion, philosophy, or education. In extreme cases, they are self–righteous.

Saturn in Capricorn

Saturn is strong here, bestowing strong ambition for power, to get ahead in the world. Often these people choose politics, science or business as their profession. They are usually stern, appear to be cold and calculating to others (although they may not be that way at all in their hearts), strict disciplinarians, hard working, task masters. This is definitely a leadership placement unless the rest of the horoscope does not support it. These people have the personal drive to overcome just about any adversity. If the person is honest, success is almost assured. If dishonest, the person may succeed for a while, but will most assuredly have a great fall.

Saturn in Aquarius

Often these people gravitate toward organizations because they need to work with groups of people. As with all Saturn positions, this one also has ambition and the desire to be in charge. In any case, most often they want jobs that deal with the public such as clerk in a store, sales work, politics, or championing some humanitarian cause. If Saturn is well aspected, they are honest, responsible, friendly, and have good judgment. If poorly aspected, they can be selfish and domineering and demand that others follow their rules.

Saturn in Pisces

Saturn is the karmic planet, and Pisces is the karmic sign. Together they can give a person difficulties such as: fearfulness, neuroses, linked too strongly to the past rather than living in the present. Often these people have difficulty coping with the present. Positively, they are humble, understanding, and are willing to help less fortunate people. Negatively, they can be paranoid and worry to excessiveness. If they learn to avoid so much introspection, they can overcome much of the drawbacks that go with this Saturn placement. As employees, they either are selfless workers, or shiftless bums, depending on Saturn's aspects.

URANUS

Uranus spends about seven years in each sign. As a result, its sign placement is more indicative of a generation of people than it is of individual traits. Covered here are a few keywords for potential individual traits associated with the Uranus signs placements. Uranus's house placements are much more individualized than its sign placements as you will see in the next chapter.

Uranus in Aries

Impulsiveness, temper, tactless. Sometimes violent, fanatical.

Uranus in Taurus

Determined, sometimes stubborn. Sometimes gifted artistic and musical talents. Interest in electronics and accounting.

Uranus in Gemini

Restless, sometimes eccentric, impractical, and strange thinking patterns. Sometimes poor relationships with brothers, sisters, and neighbors.

Uranus in Cancer

Dislikes parental authority. Like unique architecture. Fill their homes with gadgets and electronic items. May be interested in communal living. Much psychic sensitivity. Sometimes moody or erratic behavior.

Uranus in Leo

Strong willpower and creative ability. Develops new concepts in art and theater. Dislikes conformity, preferring to set their own rules. Sometimes they can be extremely stubborn, insisting on having their own way, making it difficult to get along with them.

Uranus in Virgo

Original, yet practical, ideas with regard to work. Probably many changes in employment. Sometimes erratic health problems.

Uranus in Libra
Seeks to change existing laws. Often have telepathic ability. Sometimes have great difficulty getting along in marriage or other kinds of partnerships because they often are not willing to accept mutual responsibility.

Uranus in Scorpio
Powerful emotions. Intolerant of laziness. Sometimes violent temper and will do whatever they feel they have to do (including being destructive) to achieve what they want.

Uranus in Sagittarius
Strong desire to integrate science and religion with the occult, astrology. Sometimes they are skeptics or agnostics. Curious about foreign cultures.

Uranus in Capricorn
Strong ambitions and desire to succeed. At times, can be overambitious. Likes to do away with the old and replace it with something new.

Uranus in Aquarius
Powerful position for Uranus. Intuitive insights, seeks truth. Strong willpower and strong desire for independence. Deep concern for humanity. Reformers, usually working within groups. In some cases, extreme eccentricity.

Uranus in Pisces
Seeks liberation from the past. Continual struggle to overcome the past and evolve to a higher spirituality. Sometimes they try to avoid facing unpleasant situations. Sometimes they are impractical or even deceptive.

NEPTUNE

Neptune spends about 13 years in each sign. As a result its sign placement is more indicative of a generation of people than of individual traits. A few individual potential trait keywords are given here for Neptune's sign placements. Neptune's house placement is much more individualized than its sign placement as you will see in the next chapter.

Neptune in Aries
Spiritual creativity. Sometimes spiritual pride and egotism.

Neptune in Taurus
Visionary insights. Sometimes preoccupation with money and possessions.

Neptune in Gemini
Active imaginations. Sometimes superficial values.

Neptune in Cancer
Strong psychic abilities. Sometimes overly sentimental.

Neptune in Leo
Strong artistic talents. Sometimes suffer from self-delusion.

Neptune in Virgo
Sometimes psychosomatic illness. Dwells too much on unimportant matters.

Neptune in Libra:
Blind conformity without evaluating the worth of

the matter. Social responsibility.

Neptune in Scorpio
Loose morals. Clairvoyance.

Neptune in Sagittarius
Much foreign travel. Sometimes aimless wandering (cults, gurus, etc.).

Neptune in Capricorn
Karmic reckoning.

Neptune in Aquarius
Highly developed intuition and clairvoyance.

Neptune in Pisces
Healing ability. High spiritual development.

PLUTO

Pluto spends 248 years to make one cycle through the zodiac. Its sign placement is definitely indicative of masses of people rather than individuals. Additionally, there has been very little time to study Pluto thoroughly because it was only discovered in 1930. We will not attempt to define the influence of Pluto's sign placements with regard to individuals.

Pluto's house placement is quite important in individual charts as you will see in the next chapter.

12

Planets in the Houses

SUN

Sun in First House
Powers of leadership. Strong will and great energy and vitality. Not easily swayed by others. Great ability to overcome illness. Ambitious. These people want to feel important and will work hard to achieve it. If the Sun is afflicted with harsh aspects, there can be egotism, excessive pride, and a desire to rule rather than lead.

Sun in Second House
This shows how the person will likely earn and spend money by the sign the Sun is in while in the second house. For example, if the Sun is in Leo, the person might earn a living in the theater (or some other Leo pursuit). If the Sun is afflicted, there may be squandering of money.

Sun in Third House
Achievement through mental accomplishments. Desire for travel. Brothers, sisters, and neighbors play an important role in these people's life. If afflicted, these people can be snobs.

Sun in Fourth House

These people are proud of their homes and their heritage. Early life is usually a struggle with prosperity coming late in life. Strong interest in land and natural resources. If afflicted, inability to get along with parents or rules his/her own household as though it were property rather than people.

Sun in Fifth House

Great love of life and creative expression. These people are highly competitive and strive to be noticed. They gravitate toward the theater, arts, sports, and musical careers. They love children but often have none or very few of their own. Sometimes can be egotistical. They have happy, optimistic dispositions. They are intense lovers.

Sun in Sixth House

Delicate health and not good recuperative powers. These people seek distinction through their work and through service to others. If the Sun is afflicted they may experience long periods of unemployment which can be harmful to their self-esteem because they identify strongly with their work.

Sun in Seventh House

These people must have close personal relationships. Marriage is extremely important to them. If the Sun is well aspected, they will attract good mates and will have a good marriage. If afflicted, they attract the wrong type of mate for them which can lead to a difficult marriage. These people can be good salespersons.

Sun in Eighth House

Great interest in life's mysteries such as death and life after death. With good aspects, this Sun placement can foretell of inheritances. With poor aspects, it foretells of litigation over money matters. Sometimes this Sun indicates that the person will gain recognition or honors after death but not during their lifetime.

Sun in Ninth House
There is great interest in spiritual matters, religion, law, philosophy, and higher education. Foreign travel is often indicated. in some cases, these people are bigots, condescending, and narrow minded.

Sun in Tenth House
Great ambition to achieve positions of power and authority. Usually these people are dignified and will work hard to succeed. Managerial ability goes with this Sun position. If afflicted, there can be dictatorial behavior.

Sun in Eleventh House
Usually these people have many friends. They are interested in occult matters. Often they desire group leadership. These people are humanitarians. If the Sun is afflicted, there is a tendency to dominate others.

Sun in Twelfth House
These people direct their thoughts and energies inward rather than outward. They spend much time in self contemplation. Often they seek work in asylums, hospitals or other large institutions. By serving others, they find fulfillment. If the Sun has harsh aspects, there can be extreme shyness or neurosis.

MOON

Moon in First House
Highly impressionable; sometimes psychic. They de-

sire personal recognition and seek approval from others. They are fond of food and sometimes are overweight. They allow themselves to be greatly influenced by other people. Moody and changeable.

Moon in Second House

Good business ability. Strong need for financial security. They often work in businesses dealing with food, real estate or domestic goods.

Moon in Third House

Prone to daydreaming and flights of fantasy. Much mental dwelling on unimportant matters. Gets bored easily. Much activity with brothers and sisters. They regard neighbors as being part of their family. Strong imaginations.

Moon in Fourth House

Strong Moon position. Family relationships extremely important and influence all other aspects of the person's life. Mother especially is a strong influence. If the Moon has harsh aspects, the home life can be quite unpleasant.

Moon in Fifth House

Romance is a big thing for these people, and they often become emotionally dependent on their romantic partner. There can be family interference in romance. If the Moon has harsh aspects, these people are prone to gamble or speculate impulsively.

Moon in Sixth House

Unstable health. Sometimes psychosomatic illness. Prone to be hypochondriacs. Many changes of employment unless the Moon is in a fixed sign. These people like pets and small animals.

Moon in Seventh House

These people find emotional fulfillment through marriage or other relationships. Often they marry a father or mother figure.

Moon in Eighth House

Intense emotions and psychic sensitivity. Sometimes too much sensuality.

Moon in Ninth House

Strong spiritual and moral values, especially with regard to family and home life. These people's beliefs are based on emotion and feelings rather than on fact or logic.

Moon in Tenth House

Often come from families with high standing in the community. Careers are often influenced by women. Almost always, this Moon position foretells of prominence in public life. These people are driven by a need for recognition and prominence.

Moon in Eleventh House

There is a great need for friendships. They like people around all the time and function best in groups. They have many acquaintances, but most are likely to be superficial. Their own emotions are influenced by what other people think.

Moon in Twelfth House

The past is a great influence over these people. Many have psychic ability. They are shy and their feelings are easily hurt. If the Moon has some harsh aspects, there can be neurosis and loneliness. If the Moon has many harsh aspects, it signifies mental illness and probable institutionalization because of it.

MERCURY

Mercury in First House

These people are aware of everything around them. Logical minds. Talkative and often write a great deal. Usually very intelligent. They excel at being able to express themselves. They make good physicians, writers, secretaries, and scholars. Competitive.

Mercury in Second House

Business ability in all areas of communication. Preoccupation with money. Generally these people have original ideas.

Mercury in Third House

Generally superior intelligence. Very strong interests in all sorts of communication. Much short distance traveling. Spend much time writing letters. Good problem solvers. If Mercury has harsh aspects, there can be difficulty with contracts and agreements.

Mercury in Fourth House

These people often work out of their home. Often their parents are well educated. They will likely have a large personal library in their home. Earth sciences interest them. They may even be writers dealing with environmental problems. These people often lead a nomadic life, roaming from place to place. Many times they live in trailers.

Mercury in Fifth House

Here you find playwrights and drama critics. Forceful and dramatic speakers and writers. They like mental games. This is a good placement for school teachers, especially for the primary grades. If Mercury is afflicted, the person would be wise to avoid speculation in the stock market or similar financial speculation.

Mercury in Sixth House

Methodical, efficient people who usually pursue highly specialized work that involves exacting attention to detail. Favorable for science, engineering, and medical careers.

Mercury in Seventh House

Adept at working and communicating effectively with other people in a partnership or cooperative type of work. They make good mediators and counselors. They need marriage partners who are intelligent and well educated.

Mercury in Eighth House

There is interest in matters dealing with death, inheritance, taxes, insurance. These are usually secretive people. They love intrigue. These people never forget a wrong performed against them. Their own death is often caused by respiratory diseases or by disorders of the nervous system.

Mercury in Ninth House

There is much interest in law, religion, philosophy, and higher education. Much interest in foreign cultures and travel. Good position for lawyers, especially trial lawyers. Also good position for professors and teachers. If Mercury is afflicted, there can be opinionated snobbery.

Mercury in Tenth House

Good organizers and planners. Leadership ability. Excellent position for all work dealing with the public.

Many politicians and writers have this Mercury in their natal chart. Also a good position for publishing, lecturing, teaching professions.

Mercury in Eleventh House

These people are interested in group communication. They function at their best in concert with others; there are no "loners" here. Most often they have some affiliation with astrology, humanitarian causes, scientific investigations, and various occult matters. in extreme cases, they are eccentric and impractical.

Mercury in Twelfth House

They make decisions based more on feelings than on facts or logic. These are shy people who rarely say what is really on their mind. There can be great psychic ability and awareness. If Mercury is afflicted, there can be mental illness or neurotic behavior.

VENUS

Venus in First House

Love of beautiful clothes. These people are charming, have poise and grace, and are friendly and likable. In a woman's chart, this indicates physical beauty. There can be talent in various art forms. Usually indicates a happy childhood.

Venus in Second House

Love of wealth and the things wealth can buy. Love of beautiful material objects in general. These people seek wealthy partners or those with social status. Women are usually extravagant. Men usually spend too much on their women friends. These people are usually able to get the help they seek.

Venus in Third House

Good communicators. Much travel, especially short distance. Love of literature. Often they communicate through newspapers or other published means.

Venus in Fourth House

Love of home and family life. They like to entertain in the home and cook for their friends. Home is usually a place of beauty. Much happiness through their parents and usually inherit from the parents. Love of gardening.

Venus in Fifth House

Love of life. Romance is vitally important to them. Optimistic. These people are often talented in the performing arts. Usually these people are well liked. Deep love of children, and their children are likely to be quite attractive and talented.

Venus in Sixth House

Love of work. Social and romantic opportunities through their work. Harmonious relationships with co-workers and boss. Like to work in beautiful, pleasant surroundings. These people sometimes are clothing designers. Deep affection for pets and small animals.

Venus in Seventh House

Love of personal relationships. Get along very well with other people. They usually marry at a young age and most often have good marriages. They rarely end up in court.

Venus in Eighth House

Extremely intense emotions, which can easily get out of control and develop into jealousy or possessiveness. in general, this is not a good placement for Venus. This does, however, indicate financial gain through marriage and/or inheritance.

Venus in Ninth House

Love of religion and philosophy. Often there are long journeys primarily for pleasure. Most likely will meet their romantic and social contacts through churches, universities, or in foreign countries. Relationship with in-laws is usually harmonious and profitable.

Venus in Tenth House

Great social ambition. Most often will choose a profession related to the arts. Will seek marriage to someone who has social status and/or wealth. Good relationships with employers and other authorities. Much success in dealing with the opposite sex.

Venus in Eleventh House

Marriage partner is met through group activities. Many warm friendships through group activities. Many friends of the opposite sex. These people almost always achieve their hopes and dreams.

Venus in Twelfth House

Love of solitude and peace. Secret love affairs. Shyness that can lead to loneliness or frustration in romantic situations. Feelings are easily hurt. Great compassion for the troubles of others.

MARS

Mars in First House

Self-confidence. Courage. Leadership ability. Aggressive. Great energy and stamina; these people can accomplish twice as much as most people. These people are participants in life—not bystanders. Often the men are physically rugged. If Mars is heavily afflicted, they will likely be combative or even violent. If there is self-discipline, these people usually achieve high goals.

Mars in Second House

These people strive to achieve financial gain.They prefer to be in business for themselves rather than work for others. They will fight to protect their possessions, but will readily give away possessions to gain favors from others. If Mars is afflicted, they are often dishonest and will pick fights. These are competitive people.

Mars in Third House

Mentally alert and quick thinking. Sometimes very assertive, hence they make good newspaper reporters or commentators. Tendency to jump to conclusions without sufficient facts. These people often work with machinery in various fields of communication or in the transportation industry. If Mars is poorly aspected, they can be reckless drivers who have little concern for other drivers. If heavily afflicted, they can be argumentive, have trouble with contracts, or get along poorly with brothers, sisters, and neighbors.

Mars in Fourth House

These people like to dominate the home and family, often causing quarrels and unpleasantness. They are do-it-yourself repairmen at home. Often these people work hard to improve the environment. Strong constitution and much energy even in old age. If Mars is heavily afflicted, there is danger of fire, theft, and accidents in the home.

Mars in Fifth House

These people vigorously pursue love, sex, pleasure,

and games. Athletes often have this Mars placement. They like to work with children because it gives them a sense of power and authority. If Mars is heavily afflicted by harsh aspects, there is danger that their own children may experience death or serious accidents. Also with heavy afflictions, there can be out of wedlock pregnancy.

Mars in Sixth House

These are hard working skilled people who usually have a profession that requires the use of tools or machinery. Some examples: surgeons, mechanics, mechanical engineers, equipment operators, etc. These people have no patience for lazy workers. If Mars is afflicted, they are in danger of injury in their work and should exercise extreme caution at all times.

Mars in Seventh House

These people are aggressive and choose aggressive marriage business and marriage partners. They can accomplish much if Mars is not afflicted. If afflicted, there will be serious disagreements with business partners and likely divorce from marriage partner. These people frequently become sales persons or public relations persons, and they are always aggressive.

Mars in Eighth House

Emotional intensity and strong desires, especially sexual desires. Sometimes there is psychic ability. Often indicates sudden death, a violent one if Mars is afflicted. If Mars is heavily afflicted, there are usually criminal tendencies. There is aggressiveness with other people's money.

Mars in Ninth House

These people are crusaders, promoting social reform,

championing some cause, trying to sway others to their way of thinking. They back up their beliefs with action, thus often achieving success. They like adventure and foreign travel. Fire and brimstone evangelists are typical of this Mars placement. Frequently they are narrow-minded and overly aggressive, which gains them much resentment from others. They often condemn those who have beliefs different from theirs.

Mars in Tenth House

This is a powerful position for Mars. There is executive ability, much initiative, strong desire to achieve high goals. These people very frequently become famous (or notorious in some cases). Military, business, and political leaders often have this placement. In extreme cases, their quest for power is pursued with no regard for right or wrong. If Mars is heavily afflicted, there can be sudden reversals of fortune, usually due to unethical or dishonest dealings.

Mars in Eleventh House

These people are aggressively involved with group activities. Their friends are almost always aggressive and masculine or behave in a masculine way. This placement produces revolutionaries if Mars is heavily afflicted. With Mars afflicted, these people will most likely die, or be seriously injured, in the company of friends or could be the cause of a friend's death.

Mars in Twelfth House

These people are secretive in order to avoid opposition from other people. They gravitate toward work in large institutions where they can lose their identity. These people need to be open and honest. There is danger of being incarcerated in prison or institutions if Mars is heavily afflicted.

JUPITER

Jupiter in First House

These are the boy scouts and girl scouts—honest, trustworthy, optimistic, friendly, truthful, kind, well liked, helpful, dignified (especially in later years), confident, popular. There is leadership ability here, especially in education, religion, and social organizations. These people are always protected; even when things look grim, help will come in the nick of time. There is some possibility of becoming obese, especially in later years.

Jupiter in Second House

Exceptional business ability and good fortune in money matters. If Jupiter is badly afflicted, the money will be frittered away. Businesses associated with this placement are: hospitals and institutions, domestic products, food, real estate, publishing, travel, education, psychology.

Jupiter in Third House

There is interest in publishing, writing, religion, teaching, philosophy, communications, and both long distance and short distance travel. If Jupiter is afflicted by Mars or Uranus, there is danger of accidents while traveling, but the person usually will not be seriously hurt. There is good relationships with siblings and neighbors unless Jupiter is afflicted.

Jupiter in Fourth House

Harmony in family life. Good fortune in the last half of life. Usually come from good families. Often the home is large and there are many family members. There is likelihood of inheritance from other family members. If Jupiter is heavily afflicted, family members can be a burden and cause large expenses.

Jupiter in Fifth House

Great fondness for children, and often these people become teachers and counselors for children. Their own children are usually quite fortunate and achieve honors. There is happiness in romance unless Jupiter is afflicted. In addition to education, these people are interested in sports and the arts.

Jupiter in Sixth House

These people strive to make a practical contribution to society. They are especially adept at various healing skills (both mental and physical). Christian Science practitioners are typical of this Jupiter position. These people are well liked and respected for their work skills. There can be laziness and a holier-than-thou attitude if Jupiter is afflicted.

Jupiter in Seventh House

Good fortune through marriage and business partnerships. These people are kind and friendly. They often marry someone with money or social status. There is ability in sales, law, public relations, and negotiating.

Jupiter in Eighth House

Death is usually peaceful and due to natural causes unless Jupiter is badly afflicted. These people usually gain through inheritance, joint finances, or insurance. They are attracted to businesses associated with death and taxes.

Jupiter in Ninth House

These people generally seek as much education as they possibly can. Often these people are clergy or have other positions associated with religion. They are usually very understanding. They like travel, especially foreign. Other professions are likely to be in publishing or education.

Jupiter in Tenth House

Success and prominence in the profession in the later part of life. There is much professional ambition, honesty, and reliability. These people have good reputations and often have positions in the public domain. These are good managers and executives. They have a good chance of acquiring wealth in the latter part of their life. This position also confers a great deal of protection for the person.

Jupiter in Eleventh House

Involvement with group activities, especially humanitarian and charitable organizations. Generally kind and well liked. These people are usually generous and willing to lend a helping hand to friends and organizations. If Jupiter has many harsh aspects, the person may lack a sense of responsibility and will probably use friends for their own personal gain.

Jupiter in Twelfth House

These people often give their time and money quietly behind the scenes to charitable causes. They also like seclusion where they can meditate, pray, or study. Sometimes there is psychic ability. If Jupiter is badly afflicted, these people may themselves become charity cases or inmates of institutions. There is a tendency to dwell on fantasies. If well aspected, this Jupiter brings help in times of crises.

SATURN

Saturn in First House

These people usually appear to others to be cold, remote, humorless, and excessively cheap. They are, however, very serious minded and hard working and can be loyal friends. They do need to learn to love and to lighten up to achieve happiness. If Saturn is heavily afflicted, these people have a "rough row to hoe" - usually a harsh childhood, frustrations, hostility, continual obstacles in their path through life.

Saturn in Second House
These people must work hard for a living. If Saturn is well aspected, they will most likely achieve financial success (wealth), which is always their goal because they have a deep seated fear of poverty. If Saturn is poorly aspected, they will gain very little, or nothing, for all their hard work. These people are usually shrewd in business and get their money's worth. They are always frugal, and sometimes miserly.

Saturn in Third House
These people often seek careers where science or mathematics are involved because they have methodical, practical, disciplined minds. They are not prone to travel very much, and then only for business purposes. They may have problems with their siblings or neighbors if Saturn is afflicted.

Saturn in Fourth House
In their later years, these people often become confined to their home either by choice or by necessity. They must have a home, especially in later years, to feel secure and they consciously work to have that security. Often there is emotional isolation or separation from family members. Their home and family often impose heavy burdens on these people.

Saturn in Fifth House
Women with this placement can have difficulty in giving birth. Career choices often concern the entertain-

ment industry, stocks and investments, schools, and sometimes politics or business management. They often have romances with older persons. If Saturn is heavily afflicted, they often have disappointment in love, do not like or get along with children, and may even become impotent or frigid due to emotional blocks.

Saturn in Sixth House

Efficient, serious, skilled, hard working people. They have analytical minds with a bent toward engineering, mechanics, medicine, science, or anything requiring precision and attention to detail. They are health conscious, but may suffer from chronic illness if Saturn has harsh aspects. They are respected by their co-workers unless Saturn is harshly aspected, in which case they have unsatisfactory relationships.

Saturn in Seventh House

This is a strong Saturn placement that bestows a strong sense of responsibility and justice. They seek serious minded partners and usually marry later in life. The marriage, or other type partnerships, will be enduring if Saturn is well aspected, and fraught with problems if it is harshly aspected.

Saturn in Eighth House

They often fear death and can have dreams and psychic experiences that disturb them psychologically. If Saturn is well aspected, they can be successful in handling other people's money, insurance, corporate finances, inheritance and taxes. If Saturn is badly afflicted, they will most likely be involved in litigation or other problems in these same areas.

Saturn in Ninth House

Their business is likely to deal with teaching, publishing, law, religion and travel. Their own personal travel, however, will be for business, rarely for pleasure. They have high standards and tend to follow conventional lines of thought and behavior. If Saturn is afflicted, they are prone to be narrow-minded.

Saturn in Tenth House

This placement promises great success, achievement, public recognition, and honors when Saturn is well aspected. It also promises public disgrace and a fall from the heights of achievement when Saturn is afflicted or when the person fails to conduct him/herself with integrity. This is a good placement for politicians and business executives.

Saturn in Eleventh House

These people seek out others who are powerful and influential in order to advance their own interests. They work in and through groups and organizations. They gravitate toward friendships with older, serious minded people.

Saturn in Twelfth House

These people rarely get recognized for their work or contributions. Then tend to remain in the background and hide themselves in large institutions either as workers or as inmates, depending on whether Saturn is well aspected or poorly aspected. They often have secret enemies who work to bring about their downfall.

URANUS

Uranus in First House

These people cannot stand routine work or a routine lifestyle. They must have constant change, excitement, and adventure, and they have very little regard for security. Freedom is extremely important to them. They tend to be eccentric, unconventional, a skewed behavior that swings to extremes (never in moderation), unpredictable, and if Uranus is well aspected they have superior intelligence or genius. More often than not, they are tall.

Uranus in Second House:

They have an unconventional sense of value, often earning money in unusual ways. Their finances are unsettled, suddenly making or losing money. They are borrowers and lenders. Frequently they earn money with inventions, electronics, or scientific fields. If Uranus is afflicted, they don't pay their debts and have conflict about it.

Uranus in Third House:

Exceptionally intuitive people who often receive ideas and information through sudden insights. They seek intellectual and unusual friendships. They have little regard for the opinions of others, preferring to dig out the facts for themselves. This placement often produces writers of astrological, occult, and scientific works. If Uranus is afflicted, they are fidgety, restless, impractical, and constantly change their opinions.

Uranus in Fourth House:

There will be lots of gadgets and electronic devices in their home, and their home life will be unusual. They use the home for meetings for occult activities or other group meetings. Parents and family do not have a strong, binding effect on these people. There will most likely be many sudden changes of residence.

Uranus in Fifth House:

In general, love life is unstable unless Uranus is well

aspected. There are sudden romances that terminate just as suddenly. Romantic partners are eccentric, strange, or unusual in some way. Their children can be extraordinarily gifted if Uranus is well aspected, but can have abnormalities or peculiar problems if poorly aspected. If Uranus is heavily afflicted, there will likely be anti-social behavior.

Uranus in Sixth House

These people gravitate toward high technology fields in occupations such as programming and engineering. Usually they have harmonious relationships at work, and will often quit a job if they are not satisfied with their co-worker relationships. If Uranus is afflicted, they will have explosive relationships with co-workers.

Uranus in Seventh House

Long term marriage is rare, and divorce is fairly common because these people want freedom and independence above all. They cannot stand to have a partner who they feel out shines them. Their relationships with people are at either of two extremes: extremely close or superficial with rapid turnover of people. Other people are confused by their unpredictable behavior.

Uranus in Eighth House

There is much interest in the occult and psychic matters, and often they possess considerable psychic ability. Their death is most likely to be sudden, and via an accident if Uranus is afflicted. They often have sudden changes in fortune—rags to riches and vise versa—depending on how Uranus is aspected.

Uranus in Ninth House

They have unorthodox views and interests such as

astrology, reincarnation, or strange religious beliefs. If Uranus is well aspected they can be highly spiritual and philosophical—a guru for example. If poorly aspected they may belong to fanatical cults and espouse views that are worthless and impractical.

Uranus in Tenth House

Their political views are ultra-liberal or radical— never conservative. They have leadership ability in humanitarian, scientific, occult, electronic, and astrology fields. They are prone to sudden changes of fortune. There may be many job changes and difficulty in getting along with those in authority. They want total freedom in their job with no one telling them what to do.

Uranus in Eleventh House

These are definitely humanitarian people who are truth seekers and who have no respect for tradition or the status quo. They like humanitarian group activities. They are usually unwilling to be bound to just one relationship. If Uranus is afflicted, they will probably suffer treachery from persons they thought were friends.

Uranus in Twelfth House

They are highly developed psychics if Uranus is heavily aspected with favorable aspects. They spend much time in introspection and meditation. If Uranus is afflicted, they can be neurotic and suffer delusions. They often join secret organizations and they prefer to work behind the scenes where they are not noticed.

NEPTUNE

Neptune in First House

These people must avoid the use of drugs and alcohol, especially if Neptune is afflicted, because it will most likely result in self-delusion, confusion, tendency to drift aimlessly through life with no achievement or success, and in extreme cases it can result in possession by an undesirable astral entity. If well aspected, these people have highly developed intuition and clairvoyant faculties, and can have inspired mystical visions. Some typical occupations would be: movie or television camera person, hypnotist, composers, musicians, artists.

Neptune in Second House

These people are idealistic about money and often donate their money to spiritual and humanitarian causes. They frequently use their intuition to amass large sums of money only to let it slip through their fingers and mysteriously disappear. They are often extravagant. If Neptune is afflicted, they will be lazy, impractical, and their finances will be a mess; they may even depend on others for support.

Neptune in Third House

They have very intuitive minds and good visualization ability. They gravitate toward occult subjects, often as writers. They usually have nicknames or pseudonyms. If Neptune is afflicted, they are prone to fantasize, daydream, and learning difficulties.

Neptune in Fourth House

They live, or would like to live, near the water. There is strong emotional ties with the home and parents. Frequently one of the parents is psychic. There can be nervous disorders, especially later in life, if Neptune is afflicted.

Neptune in Fifth House

Their children will likely be intuitive and very sensitive. They, themselves, have great intuitive insight and artistic expression in music, art, and the stock market. If Neptune is afflicted, it is often better if they never marry or have children for there can be great psychological problems, illegitimate children, and broken families.

Neptune in Sixth House

Work is a spiritual experience for these people. They are most interested in medicine, spiritual healing, health foods, and other kinds of healing. Often they are able to communicate psychically with animals. If Neptune is afflicted, they may be hypochondriacs or mentally ill. Also, if afflicted, there can be much unemployment and unreliability.

Neptune in Seventh House

These people have great intuitive awareness of others and thus are greatly affected by the moods and feelings of others. They usually have a strong psychic link with their marriage partner. These people more often than not have artistic and musical talent; at the very least, an appreciation of art.

Neptune in Eighth House

There are usually psychic tendencies, and they have a special interest in communicating with the dead. There is often strange things going on with regard to their partner's money such as secretive things or deception. If Neptune is afflicted, there can be problems concerning income tax fraud, insurance fraud, or fraudulent circumstances surrounding death.

Neptune in Ninth House

There is an interest in cults and mystical organizations. These people are very impressionable. If Neptune is afflicted, they become misguided in their spiritual beliefs and practices.

Neptune in Tenth House

Intuition plays an important role in their chosen career. Astrologers, clergy, psychiatrists frequently have this Neptune position. If Neptune is well aspected they will usually achieve honor in their work. If poorly aspected, they will achieve dishonor.

Neptune in Eleventh House

Unusual, idealistic friends and group associations. They are generous and helpful to their friends and have a close spiritual rapport with them. If Neptune is afflicted, they must use great care in selecting friends because there is an excellent chance of their friends being deceptive and even becoming enemies.

Neptune in Twelfth House

A strong intuitive link with cosmic consciousness. They prefer privacy. Often they remember previous incarnations and are able to bring forth wisdom from those previous experiences into the current lifetime. If Neptune is well aspected they can possess healing ability and other psychic abilities which they use beneficially. If badly aspected, they have mental confusion, neurosis, and misguided use of their innate psychic ability.

PLUTO

Pluto in First House

These people are so extremely individualistic and non-conforming that it is very difficult to get along with them in marriage, business, or other close relationships. If Pluto is conjunct the ascendant and heavily aspected there are strong clairvoyant and psychic abilities. Usually these people have strong willpower.

Pluto in Second House

Powerful drive and ambition to get money and other material resources. Often their quest for money involves other people's money. If Pluto is well aspected they will have considerable resourcefulness in achieving wealth. If Pluto is afflicted, they will most likely be greedy and selfish, causing them to lose friends and probably getting them involved in litigation over money matters.

Pluto in Third House

These people have scientific ability and much mental resourcefulness. They are highly opinionated and will not change their minds unless strong factual evidence convinces them that they were wrong. They are secretive and often deal in secret transactions. When they travel, it is most often for secret or strange reasons, and they are in danger of accidents during travel. This would be a good position for spies, undercover agents, diplomatic couriers, etc.

Pluto in Fourth House

These people tend to dominate their own home and domestic life, sometimes alienating other family members. Sometimes there is interest in the occult, which usually develops late in life. They are interested in the earth, geology, and sometimes mining.

Pluto in Fifth House

These people have much creative power which can be expressed through art or love; often they have talented children. If Pluto is afflicted, they tend to sexual excesses and will dominate or be dominated by their romantic partner. Also if afflicted, they may be overly severe toward children, and are likely to lose money if they indulge in speculation.

Pluto in Sixth House

People who work on government atomic energy projects often have Pluto in this position. Other professions may be junk and salvage or secretarial. Whatever they do, they seek to improve their work and working conditions. If Pluto is badly afflicted, they can be very difficult to work with, thus causing employment problems.

Pluto in Seventh House

These people have a tendency to dominate or be dominated by others. In marriage or other partnerships they tend to be attracted to strong willed, dominating types of people. This is a good position for judges, psychologists, and lawyers.

Pluto in Eighth House

They have powerful wills, sometimes combined with considerable psychic ability. They have great strength and resourcefulness in a crisis. If Pluto is afflicted, they will have problems with insurance, taxes, other people's money, or inheritance.

Pluto in Ninth House

Strong spiritual leadership ability is evident here. They have no tolerance for hypocrisy. If Pluto is afflicted, they can be religious fanatics who try to change everyone to their own way of thinking.

Pluto in Tenth House

These people are leaders who have strong will power and a drive to succeed. They know how to wield power wisely and effectively. However, if Pluto is afflicted, they become dictatorial and put their personal gain ahead of everything else.

Pluto in Eleventh House

They have the ability to be successful leaders of groups if Pluto is well aspected. If badly afflicted, tend to be self-serving leaders and extravagant spenders.

Pluto in Twelfth House

This is a strong occult position, conferring great intuition and understanding of life's mysteries when Pluto is well aspected. If Pluto is afflicted, there is danger of destructive psychic forces, secret enemies, or neurotic problems.

13

The Aspects

CONJUNCTIONS
NOTE: The only major aspect the Sun can have with either Mercury or Venus is a conjunction. The only major aspects that Mercury and Venus can have with each other are a conjunction or a sextile.

Sun conjunct Moon
Person combines concentration with impulsiveness. Alternates between being passive and aggressive.

Sun conjunct Mercury
This gives great mental energy and power, but if the conjunction is too close (less than 4 degrees generally) there is danger of mental burnout. These people are usually unable to see themselves as others see them.

Sun conjunct Venus
They love life and are usually optimistic and cheerful. Sometimes a little conceited. There is talent in art and music. They express themselves well.

Sun conjunct Mars

This confers great willpower and courage. Tendency to be aggressive and self-assertive.

Sun conjunct Jupiter

Pleasing personalities. Generous and optimistic. They attract good luck. Can usually win others over to their way of thinking or doing. Enthusiastic.

Sun conjunct Saturn

They have great self-discipline which they need because they encounter many frustrations. They gain only by hard work—nothing comes easy or for free.

Sun conjunct Uranus

To others, these people often seem to be eccentric and unpredictable because they act suddenly, decisively and with power. This is because they can see and understand things that others do not readily perceive because these people have well developed innate psychic ability. Often these people are geniuses.

Sun conjunct Neptune

This also is a psychic aspect. They can be genuinely inspired or be self-deluded, depending on the rest of the horoscope.

Sun conjunct Pluto

This is an extremely powerful psychic aspect, giving the person enormous energy and power. They understand cosmic law and power and know how to use it.

Sun conjunct Ascendant

These are strong, healthy people who rarely get sick, and if they do get sick they recuperate rapidly. Powerful people who are the masters of their lives and environment.

Sun conjunct Midheaven

These people exert great influence through their careers and personal reputations. They are attracted to public life or politics. More often than not, they gain some sort of fame.

Moon conjunct Mercury

They spend much thought concerning their families and home life. Sometimes they are overly sensitive to criticism.

Moon conjunct Venus

Usually successful in love. They make good diplomats. They express their emotions through art or beauty. Women with this aspect display their creativity through culinary skills or in beautiful clothing.

Moon conjunct Mars

Prone to fits of anger; temper tantrums in children. Whatever they do, they feel and act with emotional intensity. Their actions are based more on emotion than on reason. They can be dangerous enemies because emotion blinds them to common sense.

Moon conjunct Jupiter

These are generous, sympathetic people who are concerned about doing something good in the world. They are usually trustworthy. They often affiliate themselves with religious or educational causes. Emotional attachment to home and family.

Moon conjunct Saturn
These people are usually regarded as wet blankets because they are dour, humorless, and seem to have no joy. Too often their emotions are strongly linked to the past and to memories rather than to the present. They usually are hard, self-disciplined workers. They are practical and have common sense.

Moon conjunct Uranus
These people gravitate toward strange and unusual experiences. Moody, they have sudden changes or emotional swings and are unpredictable. Good intuition and imaginative powers go with this aspect. Their family life is often quite unusual.

Moon conjunct Neptune
These people tend to be psychic, and there often are religious and spiritual tendencies. There can be artistic or musical ability. Sometimes they have prophetic dreams.

Moon conjunct Pluto
They deliberately precipitate drastic changes in their or in their family's life. They have strong wills and intense feelings. Quite often there are psychic tendencies. They tend to be overbearing, thus driving people from them.

Moon conjunct Ascendant
These people tend to appear to be feminine and have feminine behavior, thus it is a more favorable position for women than for men. They are highly impressionable, and their childhood experiences have an exceptionally strong influence on them throughout life.

Moon conjunct Midheaven
Usually these people are in the public eye and are

popular. There can sometimes be gain through wealthy women. Often these people are connected with a family business. This position favors entertainers, politicians, and businesses that deal with homes or domestic products.

Mercury conjunct Venus

This aspect bestows literary talent, grace in expression in both speech and writing, and natural diplomatic ability. These people also have mathematical and scientific talent. In extreme cases, they can be fickle.

Mercury conjunct Mars

These people love controversy, debates, competition, and mental challenge. They have keen, energetic minds. They can make good reporters. They love to express themselves, making them naturals for politics.

Mercury conjunct Jupiter

They are usually broadminded and confident. They tend toward occupations where they can influence others through their mental abilities and speaking abilities. For example, clergy, politicians, lecturers, teachers.

Mercury conjunct Saturn

This aspect bestows a disciplined mind that is logical and precise. They are good planners. They work hard and leave no stone unturned in their quest for success. They also make good architects, engineers, draftspersons and related professions.

Mercury conjunct Uranus

These people are often geniuses. Their minds are exceptionally quick and original. Often they pursue careers in electronics. They are very independent, and sometimes too independent. Sometimes they are hard to get along with.

Mercury conjunct Neptune

These people are dreamers, and in extreme cases live in a dream world to the exclusion of reality. They often have psychic ability. Sometimes they can be deceitful. They have powerful imaginations. Photography is often a good profession, or hobby, for these people.

Mercury conjunct Pluto

These are truth seekers, and they use their willpower and penetrating minds to get to the bottom of things. They love to delve into secrets and flush out the truth. This is a good aspect for detectives or other type investigators. In some cases, they can be overbearing.

Mercury conjunct Ascendant

These people have exceptional intelligence. They tend to talk too much, which sometimes annoys others. They use logic in all their thinking processes.

Mercury conjunct Midheaven

Most often their profession will be in some field of communications such as newspaper work, free-lance writer, radio announcer, etc. Other favorable occupations are teachers, librarians, secretaries, scientists, work for the telephone company, or various sorts of clerks.

Venus conjunct Mars

Basically, this is a sensual aspect. It bestows passion, physical love desires, artistic expression of love or sexual connotations. In its highest expression, it is a generous, loving outpouring of help to others. In its most base expression, it is raw sexual exploitation.

Venus conjunct Jupiter

This can bring so much ease and good fortune into the person's life that they become lazy and unappreciative; however a strong Saturn in the chart negates this, bringing out the best qualities. These people are usually quite generous, and they love to bring joy to others.

Venus conjunct Saturn

An excellent aspect to have in a chart, it bestows high quality talent for music and the arts. Practical and generous, these people have a strong sense of justice, harmony, and fair play. If these people feel they are unloved, they often become extremely depressed.

Venus conjunct Uranus

They have sudden attractions and shifts of affection. Often they confuse friendship and romantic love. Seldom can they devote their love to just one person. Their love life is almost always in a state of flux and change.

Venus conjunct Neptune

At its highest expression, this aspect bestows a pure, spiritual love that borders on being divine. At its lowest expression, it foretells of romantic dreamers who are a burden to others and who are often unreliable and deceptive.

Venus conjunct Pluto

The positive side borders on being divine. The negative side borders on perversion. This aspect does bestow generous amounts of talent, especially for music, drama, and opera.

Venus conjunct Ascendant

This aspect bestows physical beauty and attractiveness. It also confers grace, charm, and harmony. In extreme cases, the person becomes infatuated with their own attractiveness. Sometimes they are socially aggressive.

Venus conjunct Midheaven

These people seek to improve their status. Women sometimes promote their careers by charming those in authority. This aspect especially favors those who work in the arts or in public relations.

Mars conjunct Jupiter

These people believe in themselves, sometimes to the point of being fanatical about it. They relentlessly pursue whatever goal they consider to be worthwhile, and they never accept "NO" for an answer. They have a great amount of energy and enthusiasm.

Mars conjunct Saturn

Unless this conjunction is well aspected by other planets, there will be anger, violence, and resentment. If badly aspected, this conjunction will bestow destructive and criminal tendencies. These people do have exceptional capacity for hard work, endurance, and courage. This aspect favors military careers.

Mars conjunct Uranus

These people are rebels and revolutionaries. They have courage, but usually lack good judgment. They seek to change things suddenly, and usually by drastic, unacceptable means. Their very nature puts a great strain on their nervous system. This aspects carries with it a propensity for accidents.

Mars conjunct Neptune

This aspect confers susceptibility to poisoning, drug reactions, and infectious diseases. These people almost always have strong psychic abilities, especially healing abilities. Sometimes they have lofty goals that are unrealistic.

Mars conjunct Pluto

This aspect bestows more than a normal amount of power, energy, willpower and courage. They have no fear of death or danger. In poorly developed people, there will likely be violent and criminal behavior.

Mars conjunct Ascendant

These people are forceful and aggressive. They are basically leaders, and they leave their mark wherever they go. They can accomplish a great deal if they master the art of diplomacy. Otherwise, they just make people angry. They tend to plunge into things without giving it much forethought.

Mars conjunct Midheaven

These people are highly ambitious and they desire to become important and prominent in their professional lives. They are goal oriented, and they expend great energy to achieve their goals. Political and military careers benefit from this aspect.

Jupiter conjunct Saturn

This aspect comprises opposing forces—the optimism and ease of Jupiter with the gloom and hardship of Saturn. The usual result is that the person must shoulder heavy burdens throughout life but has an element of help and protection when the going gets the roughest. They are serious minded, but optimistic up to a point; sustained disappointments can kill their optimism.

Jupiter conjunct Uranus

This aspect brings sudden and unusual benefits and advantages to the person. These people usually oppose the traditional or established way of doing things.

Jupiter conjunct Neptune

There is a tendency for extreme idealism, often accompanied by lack of self-discipline and lack of practicality. Often they promise more than they can deliver. Sometimes there is considerable psychic ability. They have great imagination.

Jupiter conjunct Pluto

This aspect confers the ability for intense concentration and strong determination to achieve goals. Usually the goals are to improve and benefit self and others. This aspect favors administrators and judges.

Jupiter conjunct Ascendant

These people have self-confidence and optimism with the ability to inspire others. If the conjunction is afflicted, they will most likely be overweight. They usually like to travel.

Jupiter conjunct Midheaven

These people have an excellent chance of attaining prominence. This aspect favors those in business, clergy persons, lawyers and associated law professions, and those in the field of education.

Saturn conjunct Uranus

Disciplined Saturn has a stabilizing effect on erratic Uranus, producing genius or near-genius intelligence that is practical, original, and creative. These people have much to offer the world. They enjoy serious studies such as mathematics, astrology, and sciences.

Saturn conjunct Neptune

If the conjunction is favorably aspected, it confers good power of concentration. It favors musicians, artists, and those engaged in secretive work. If afflicted, it can bestow all sorts of difficulties such as depression, being confined to an institution, and morbidity.

Saturn conjunct Pluto

These two powerful planets combine to endow the person with the ability to perform work that will have far-reaching and long lasting effects. Often their work will be of a secret nature. These people possess much personal power.

Saturn conjunct Ascendant

This aspect indicates difficulties in early life. It confers reliability, a serious nature, the ability to perform hard work, and usually a strong sense of responsibility.

Saturn conjunct Midheaven

These people almost always will rise to high positions in life regardless of whether they have integrity or not. With integrity, they will be a success and achieve honor. Without integrity they are guaranteed a great fall.

Uranus conjunct Neptune

This conjunction occurs about every 171 years and casts its influence on a whole generation of people rather than on individuals to any great degree. It does confer good imagination and originality.

Uranus conjunct Pluto

This occurs about every 115 years, affecting an entire generation. In individuals, it can confer some psychic ability.

Uranus conjunct Ascendant

These people are alert and individualistic. Their intuitive powers are highly developed. Often these people study and practice astrology. They insist on having personal freedom and will not tolerate interference from others.

Uranus conjunct Midheaven

This aspect favors occupations in electronics, science, physics, and astrology. They often gain fame and high positions, but there can be sudden changes in professional reputation.

Neptune conjunct Pluto

This aspect influences society in general in a subtle way to help them raise their consciousness to greater heights of love and understanding. It is so subtle that it may go unnoticed in individual horoscopes.

Neptune conjunct Ascendant

Very definitely confers psychic ability. They can have a "hypnotic" quality about them. Professional hypnotists are favored by this aspect.

Neptune conjunct Midheaven

These are not stable employees. Their best bet is to engage in professions that require creative imagination such as photography, acting, music, painting, and psychology. If the conjunction is afflicted, there is danger of public disgrace.

Pluto conjunct Ascendant

This aspect confers willpower and stamina and considerable psychic awareness.

Pluto conjunct Midheaven

This aspect all but guarantees public notice—fame or notoriety, depending on the rest of the horoscope and the individual's choices.

TRINES

Sun trine Moon

Bestows harmonious balance in the person. Insures good health and good recuperative powers. They tend to get along well with family and parents. They work well with children and have self-confidence and optimism.

Sun trine Mars

Bestows good health, physical strength, enthusiasm, leadership ability, decisiveness, courage, ambition, and willpower.

Sun trine Jupiter

This confers the same attributes as Sun trine Mars. In addition, it bestows good fortune, success, and honesty.

Sun trine Saturn

Self-discipline and good organizational ability go with this aspect. In addition, it confers practicality, honesty, good concentration powers, and a conservative disposition. These people do not waste anything.

Sun trine Uranus

These people have strong wills and the ability to tap into cosmic consciousness. They have leadership ability, creativity, and personal magnetism. Good astrologers often have this aspect.

Sun trine Neptune

Good intuition. These are usually spiritual people who express themselves in music, religion, art, or giving spiritual guidance.

Sun trine Pluto

These people have exceptional powers of concentration and an excess of energy. Sometimes they have leadership ability.

Sun trine Ascendant

Favorable aspect for a good marriage or partnerships in general. The aspect gives much energy, willpower, self-confidence, and optimism.

Sun trine Midheaven

This gives leadership ability and increases the person's chances of significant success in their career. This is a favorable position for all occupations in public life.

Moon trine Mercury

This aspect bestows common sense and good business ability. They are good communicators and often conduct business over the phone or by mail. They have very good memories.

Moon trine Venus

This aspect confers a pleasant disposition and good voice quality. It also bestows femininity and beauty. There usually is some artistic ability and good taste in general. This is a good aspect for the performing arts.

Moon trine Mars

Controlled, constructive emotions. They will fight for what they believe to be right. They combine action with imagination.

Moon trine Jupiter

These people are devoted to their home, family, and parents. They have expansive imaginations. Often they gain wealth through inheritance or through their own business acumen.

Moon trine Saturn

These people have dignity and a sense of responsibility. They have good organizational ability, are cautious, conservative, honest, and have common sense. They are shrewd in business.

Moon trine Uranus

These people are unconventional and have strong imaginations. They are original and energetic. Often they are interested in astrology and have some psychic ability.

Moon trine Neptune

This provides a considerable amount of psychic ability. They often have careers in psychology.

Moon trine Pluto

Tremendous personal power and emotional control go with this aspect. They also have great courage and determination.

Moon trine Ascendant

These people express their emotions in a constructive way. They also conduct themselves harmoniously in marriage.

Moon trine Midheaven

This aspect favors a good marriage and domestic life. It also enables the person to deal successfully with people in positions of authority.

Mercury trine Mars

This aspect confers great mental energy, mental concentration, and mental endurance. These are forceful, dramatic speakers. Often they enter law, the military, politics, or any profession that can give them opportunity for leadership.

Mercury trine Jupiter

This gives a quick mind that is tolerant and absorbs information effectively. These people have integrity and are honest. They usually like to travel.

Mercury trine Saturn

These people are loyal friends. They usually have very good manual dexterity. Their mind is well organized, and exacting work appeals to them. A good memory goes with this aspect.

Mercury trine Uranus

These people are especially suited for investigation or research work. It is also an excellent aspect for the study and practice of astrology. These are not crowd followers - they form their own opinions.

Mercury trine Neptune

This aspect bridges the logical mind with the spiritual mind to confer ability in both areas. A great deal of intuition is present. Often artistic ability is present.

Mercury trine Pluto

There is great mental ability to delve into the deepest subjects and understand them. This is an excellent aspect for physicists and those working in the nuclear energy field. It also favors writers of detective and mystery stories.

Mercury trine Ascendant

These people are quite adept at influencing others. They have sharp, quick, intelligent minds.

Mercury trine Midheaven

These people will excel in any profession that makes use of their excellent mental and communication abilities.

Venus trine Mars

This aspect is favorable for happiness in marriage and romance. These people express themselves forcefully and harmoniously. They are fun loving and usually have sex appeal.

Venus trine Jupiter

In a horoscope that is generally weak, this aspect confers laziness because things come too easy to the person. Otherwise, this aspect confers harmony and an optimistic, pleasing disposition. There usually is some creative potential here.

Venus trine Saturn

These people are usually sharp in business. They are also loyal friends and are good marriage partners. Sometimes they appear to be shy or too serious.

Venus trine Uranus

Sudden good fortune (financial especially) is associated with this aspect. These are bubbly, fun loving people. They have a great deal of sex appeal and have no difficulty in attracting romance.

Venus trine Neptune

These can be creative geniuses, especially in music and art. They are very romantic and are attracted to unusual romances or lovers.

Venus trine Pluto

These are definitely romantic people who have strong sex drives. They have an intense emotional nature and often fall in love at first sight.

Venus trine Ascendant

This aspect confers grace, harmony, attractiveness, and charm. Usually they are popular and have good marriages.

Venus trine Midheaven

Beauty, charm, and grace play a vital role for success in their occupation. If a performing artist has this aspect, some favorable public recognition is guaranteed.

Mars trine Jupiter

This aspect bestows constructive action, energy, and enthusiasm. If they are religious, they put their religious beliefs into action in the finest sense of the word.

Mars trine Saturn

These people are shrewd and work hard to satisfy their ambitions. They are skillful, daring, and have great willpower. They are able to bear heavy responsibilities, endure hardships or even face danger.

Mars trine Uranus

They are outspoken, and have nervous energy which can be difficult for others to deal with. They are resourceful and original, often pioneering new methods of doing things.

Mars trine Neptune

This aspect confers a keen sensitivity that enables them to detect insincerity in others, sensing danger, and utilizing innate psychic abilities. People who work with liquids often have this aspect.

Mars trine Pluto

These are ruthless fighters who give no quarter to defend what they believe to be right. They live life dynamically and have unbreakable willpower.

Mars trine Ascendant

These people are active, decisive, and have strong willpower.

Mars trine Midheaven

They work hard to satisfy their ambition to climb the ladder of success in their profession and to take care of their family.

Jupiter trine Saturn

This aspect bestows financial, business, and managerial abilities. It also gives honesty, common sense, and integrity. They usually have cool tempers and are dignified.

Jupiter trine Uranus

They do not like rules or constraints; they desire unrestricted freedom. Sometimes these people are genuine geniuses. They have creative ability.

Jupiter trine Neptune
This is primarily a psychic aspect, conferring the ability to interact with cosmic consciousness. They prefer to live near the water and away from urban centers.

Jupiter trine Pluto
This aspect confers tremendous creative power. They can focus their concentration, which enables them to achieve much through meditation.

Jupiter trine Ascendant
This gives an optimistic, constructive attitude. They are enthusiastic, have self-confidence, and have goodwill toward others. Usually they have harmonious marriages.

Jupiter trine Midheaven
They usually rise high in their profession due to their constructive attitude. Religion and law are favored by this aspect.

Saturn trine Uranus
This aspect is favorable for careers in science, astrology, mathematics, or leaders of groups. They have considerable willpower and are practical.

Saturn trine Neptune
These are good organizers who work best behind the scenes or in secretive type work such as investigation. They are skillful analysts, which also adapts them to working with investments.

Saturn trine Pluto
Often these people have a karmic mission to fill. They work tirelessly to achieve their goals. Good aspect for managerial positions.

Saturn trine Ascendent:
They have a dignified and conservative demeanor, and never act impulsively. They are usually trustworthy. If married, their marriage will be stable.

Uranus trine Neptune
This aspect lasts many years and affects an entire generation of people. In individual charts it confers an interest in occult matters such as astrology and psychic phenomena.

Uranus trine Pluto
This aspect lasts many years and affects an entire generation of people. In individual charts it confers an interest in life after death and reincarnation.

Uranus trine Ascendant
Often these people are clairvoyant or intuitive. They are original and have much will power. They are natural leaders who inspire others.

Uranus trine Midheaven
They usually work in "unusual" fields and achieve success, sometimes fame, which often comes suddenly and unexpectedly.

Neptune trine Pluto
This aspect lasts a very long time, affecting an entire generation. Its affects are hardly noticed in individual charts except for a tendency toward psychic matters.

Neptune trine Ascendant
They have well developed intuition. To others, they often appear to be intriguing or mysterious. Usually they have a close rapport with their marriage partner.

Neptune trine Midheaven

They use their excellent intuition effectively in their profession to solve problems and to deal with their superiors. They usually have a close rapport with their parents. They often live near water.

Pluto trine Ascendant

This confers strong will power and excellent powers of concentration. They inspire others.

Pluto trine Midheaven

These people seek leadership positions in their profession. They make strong, farsighted executives.

SEXTILES

Sun sextile Moon

This aspect endows popularity and a harmonious marriage. These people easily make friends with the opposite sex.

Sun sextile Mars

Energy, will power, decisiveness, and leadership ability are associated with this aspect. The aspect also bestows courage and ability to endure hardship.

Sun sextile Jupiter

This aspect gives a great deal of protection to the person; they rarely have any serious harm come to them. These people are also generous, confident, and optimistic and usually love to travel.

Sun sextile Saturn

These people are methodical and practical, having much patience and self-discipline. They often appear to be stern, but they are loyal friends.

Sun sextile Uranus

This aspect favors inventors because they have perceptive minds and much willpower for creating things that others are unable to do. These are magnetic people who inspire others.

Sun sextile Neptune

This aspect confers good imagination and visualization powers. They are quite sensitive to other people's emotions. They love animals.

Sun sextile Pluto

Great willpower, resourcefulness, and exceptional endurance are the marks of this aspect.

Sun sextile Ascendant

This is a good aspect for a good marriage. They are enthusiastic and creative and they express their energy harmoniously.

Sun sextile Midheaven

They express themselves well in their profession. They also have leadership ability.

Moon sextile Mercury

Neatness, cleanliness and good hygiene are associated with this aspect. These people are good communicators. They also have good memories.

Moon sextile Venus

This is favorable for all matters associated with marriage and home life. They are affectionate and are usually popular.

Moon sextile Mars

These people will fight to protect their family and home. They have a great deal of energy.

Moon sextile Jupiter

These people have a "green thumb." They are cheerful, honest, and optimistic.

Moon sextile Saturn

These people are level-headed, practical, frugal, and generally possess integrity. To other people they often appear to be dull.

Moon sextile Uranus

These people can quickly spot an opportunity, and they know how to take advantage of it. They have many female friends. Sometimes their mother is an unusual person.

Moon sextile Neptune

Psychic ability definitely comes with this aspect, and they usually know how to use it in the most spiritual and way.

Moon sextile Pluto

These people do not have a lot of "clutter" in their life. They use their minds to create the reality they want.

Moon sextile Ascendant

This confers harmony within self, between them and others in general, and within marriage.

Moon sextile Midheaven

This confers harmony in the workplace with co-workers and supervisors. If is also favorable for a harmonious home life.

Mercury sextile Venus

Grace in behavior, skill in speech and writing, and a calm disposition are marks of this aspect.

Mercury sextile Mars

These people plan what they are going to do, and then they do it. Thus, they are efficient and productive. They also have sharp minds.

Mercury sextile Jupiter

This aspect is concerned with intellectual pursuits, especially in law, religion, philosophy, and education. These people attract good things to themselves. They love to travel.

Mercury sextile Saturn

This is the premier aspect of the well disciplined mind. Their mind is precise, practical, and thinks things through thoroughly. They leave nothing to chance.

Mercury sextile Uranus

Quick, inventive minds with a good memory are marks of this aspect. They often get sudden flashes of knowledge or inspiration that enables them to solve problems.

Mercury sextile Neptune

This aspect favors photographers and writers. These people can intuitively sense what other people are up to. Often they work in secret or on secret projects.

Mercury sextile Pluto

These people are able to express themselves powerfully and effectively. They have strong will power.

Mercury sextile Ascendant

This aspect bestows the ability to communicate exceptionally well with others.

Mercury sextile Midheaven

Their ability to communicate well enables these people to do well in their profession. They also are good planners.

Venus sextile Mars

This aspect promotes harmony between the sexes. These people are usually happy and full of energy. Sometimes they become wealthy, and they are always generous with others.

Venus sextile Jupiter

This aspect bestows good fortune and an easy, comfortable life. These people are usually quite popular.

Venus sextile Saturn

This aspect confers exceptional artistic skill. They tend to be formal in their conduct. They are frugal and have good judgment in the use of money.

Venus sextile Uranus

These people fall in love suddenly and marry suddenly. They are popular and have many friends. Usually their marriage and friendships are good, bringing them good fortune.

Venus sextile Neptune

Keen artistic imagination go with this aspect. In a weak horoscope, these people are likely to be lazy and rely on help from others.

Venus sextile Pluto
This aspect favors creativity in music or art. Often their marriage seems to be preordained.

Venus sextile Ascendant
These people have grace and harmony in their self-expression. Sometimes they are peacemakers between warring factions.

Venus sextile Midheaven
These are natural diplomats. They find contentment both at home and in their profession.

Mars sextile Jupiter
These people are rarely lazy. They work strenuously to help others who are unfortunate. Often they are missionaries or engaged in some religious activity. They are undefeatable.

Mars sextile Saturn
Endurance and fortitude are the keywords here. There is a balanced blend of discipline and energy to produce practical, efficient, and tireless workers.

Mars sextile Uranus
These people know exactly what they want and they go after it with courage, fast action, and will power. These are forceful people.

Mars sextile Neptune
These people can see through the motives of others, hence they are not easily fooled. Any professions that require exceptional imagination and superior energy need

people with this aspect in their natal chart.

Mars sextile Pluto
The keywords here are great courage, iron will power, and tremendous energy.

Mars sextile Ascendant
These people earn respect because they are open and direct in their dealings.

Mars sextile Midheaven
This is a favorable aspect for both domestic and professional matters. Sometimes they use their home as the base for their professional activities.

Jupiter sextile Saturn
This aspect confers a balance between Jupiter's expansiveness, optimism, and enthusiasm and Saturn's constrictiveness, caution, practicality, and organization.

Jupiter sextile Uranus
These people make good astrologers. They are kind and altruistic. Often they are lucky in sudden, unexpected ways.

Jupiter sextile Neptune
These people often have great imagination but frequently lack the common sense to know how to use it. They tend to be gushy and overly sentimental.

Jupiter sextile Pluto
Often this aspect signifies wisdom and insight.

Jupiter sextile Ascendant
Good fortune in marriage and in dealing with the

public is indicated here. They know how to arouse enthusiasm in others, enabling them to be successful promoters for whatever enterprise they are involved with.

Jupiter sextile Midheaven
These are honest and generous people, gaining them popularity in their professional dealings. They usually have excellent reputations.

Saturn sextile Uranus
These people know how to take original or "off the wall" ideas and apply them in a practical way. They are truthful, loyal friends.

Saturn sextile Neptune
They have the ability to discipline and focus their great imaginative powers in order to produce practical results. They have great insight.

Saturn sextile Pluto
These people know how to use power wisely. The rest of the horoscope must be strong for this aspect to have much influence in the person's life.

Saturn sextile Ascendant
The keywords here are integrity, sense of responsibility, very serious disposition, reliability, self-discipline, good organization. They are respected even though they appear to be cold, and impersonal.

Saturn sextile Midheaven
These people, if they work in an established organization, will move up through the ranks because their superiors have confidence in them. They like tradition.

Uranus sextile Neptune

This aspect lasts many years, affecting an entire generation, and is usually not prominent in an individual's horoscope. There may be artistic ability.

Uranus sextile Pluto

Individuals may have sudden intuitive flashes on how to bring about constructive changes.

Uranus sextile Ascendant

These are unusual people who stand apart from the crowd. Others find them interesting. Sometimes they decide to get married suddenly, or their marriage ceremony may be a strange one.

Uranus sextile Midheaven

Often they advance professionally through the help of friends. They often entertain friends in their home.

Neptune sextile Pluto

This aspect has an extremely long duration and is not usually significant in individual horoscopes unless either Neptune or Pluto is in an angular house (1st, 4th, 7th, 10th). In this case there will be unusual scientific or psychic abilities.

Neptune sextile Ascendant

Clairvoyance or other extrasensory abilities usually accompany this aspect. Others find these people to be charming and are drawn to them magnetically.

Neptune sextile Midheaven

This confers excellent intuition in the professional life, enabling the person to sense and understand the subtle and hidden things that are going on.

Pluto sextile Ascendant

Good powers of concentration accompany this aspect. These people act decisively.

Pluto sextile Midheaven

Considerable professional skill and ambition are indicated here.

SQUARES

Sun square Moon

Creative self-expression is usually blocked by the person's family. They usually have difficulty getting along with the opposite sex. They feel insecure.

Sun square Mars

These are argumentive people who try to achieve their goals by force, thus antagonizing others. They are their own worst enemies because of their brash, aggressive behavior. Sometimes there are temper outbursts.

Sun square Jupiter

They have an unrealistic view of themselves. Usually they are very extravagant and can fritter money away faster than they can earn it. They want too much too quickly.

Sun square Saturn

This aspect puts a seemingly endless string of obstacles in the person's path, creating a life of hardship. If the person is strong, this aspect builds character. If not, it beats the person down.

Sun square Uranus

This confers erratic behavior, impractical ideas, and

lack of self-discipline. They often do not reap the rewards from their work due to their irrational behavior, which creates enemies.

Sun square Neptune

These people usually suffer from self-delusion and have a tendency to try to avoid responsibility. They frequently have secret love affairs and get involved in scandals.

Sun square Pluto

These people are forceful and domineering, creating resentment in others. They are too aggressive with the opposite sex.

Sun square Ascendant

These people have difficulty dealing with the public, with partners (including marriage). They don't seem to know how to present their true self. Usually they try to dominate others.

Sun square Midheaven

Career and family life do not run smoothly, and they conflict with each other. Usually they do not get along well with co-workers or with their boss.

Moon square Mercury

There is a tendency for problems with the nervous system or the digestive system. These are classic bores who rattle on and on about nothing worth listening to, much to the agony of their listeners.

Moon square Venus

They trust their spouse or other partners too much, and are taken advantage of by them. They get involved in unwise romantic situations. Sometimes they are just plain unlucky.

Moon square Mars
This confers volatile emotions and temper. They do not get along with women. Because they have little control over their emotions, they should avoid alcohol use.

Moon square Jupiter
These people are suckers for a sob story, and are easily "taken" for financial loss as a result. Foreign travel will likely bring them some sort of misfortune. Sometimes they are just plain lazy.

Moon square Saturn
These people are constantly "down in the dumps," moody, pessimistic, depressed, unhappy, etc. A black cloud seems to always be over their head. Often they have an inferiority complex.

Moon square Uranus
These people usually have ingenuity and great talent, but also tend toward perversity and have sudden mood swings. Often their life is plagued with misfortunes that occur suddenly, such as accidents, ill health, catastrophes, etc.

Moon square Neptune
These people live in a fantasy world that is muddled and confused. Drug and alcohol abuse are associated with this aspect. There can be psychosis or insanity. They often become social parasites.

Moon square Pluto
These people do not like to be confined by anything,

be it a job, a marriage, laws, etc. They want to force their way on others.

Moon square Ascendant

Difficulties with self-expression are associated with this aspect. It also creates problems with all relationships, including marriage.

Moon square Midheaven

They have emotional problems with parents or family. These problems spill over to interfere with their profession, causing further problems with their employer.

Mercury square Mars

These people lack tact, jump to conclusions, have one-sided reasoning, and are argumentive. As a result, they do not do well in jobs dealing with the public.

Mercury square Jupiter

These people promise more than they can deliver. They attempt things beyond their capacity. They usually have good intentions, but lack common sense. They cannot keep secrets.

Mercury square Saturn

Mental inhibition is indicated here. This can be dullness, narrow mindedness, no imagination, too wrapped up in unimportant details, or pessimism. In some cases, they are dishonest schemers.

Mercury square Uranus

A nervous disposition and harebrained ideas are indicated here. They will not accept advice from anyone. They may be perverse, make snap judgments, and be quite changeable.

Mercury square Neptune

This confers absentmindedness and general mental disorganization. These people absolutely cannot keep a secret. They have great difficulty communicating clearly.

Mercury square Pluto

They have strong will power, but usually use it in destructive ways. They are brutally blunt, saying exactly what they think in a harsh manner regardless of whether it hurts someone.

Mercury square Ascendant

They express themselves awkwardly in speech and in writing, making it difficult for them to communicate well with anyone. As a result they have constant problems in their personal life and with the world at large.

Mercury square Midheaven

They communicate poorly at home and at work, with the most serious problems occurring at work.

Venus square Mars

Problems in romance and relationships are indicated here. They tend to use, or be used by, others for sexual gratification only. They lack refinement in their social conduct. If they do not control their passions, great harm will come to them.

Venus square Jupiter

Overindulgence and laziness are the keywords here. They have no appreciation for the true values in life, and are often morally corrupt.

Venus square Saturn

Life is often exceptionally harsh for these people. Unfulfilled love and financial hardship are common. Sometimes they are obsessed with a quest for wealth, regardless of what they have to do to obtain it.

Venus square Uranus
This aspect usually indicates divorce if there is a marriage because these people will not sacrifice any personal freedom in order to make the marriage work. There can be fickleness with this aspect.

Venus square Neptune
Unwise use of affections and sex are keywords here. There can be anything from dishonesty in marriage, to perverseness, to homosexuality. If Venus or Neptune are favorably aspected by other planets, then the person will direct their sexual energy in some creative way, such as writing or art, rather than in sexual misuse.

Venus square Pluto
There is a tendency to give in to overwhelming sexual passions. Sometimes external events, such as war, disrupt personal happiness. Marriage is likely to be motivated more by material gain than by love.

Venus square Ascendant
The person may be ultra-sensitive emotionally, thus precipitating problems in the marriage. Sometimes the person has no social grace.

Venus square Midheaven
Often the person finds both their job and their home life to be dull and unfulfilling. Most likely they will not get along very well with their parents.

Mars square Jupiter

This is a very destructive aspect that may be found in the horoscopes of those who glorify war, have violent tendencies that they display under the guise of seeking social justice, who espouse fanatical religions that often use violence against those who oppose them, and so forth.

Mars square Saturn

Physical hardships, violence, broken bones, accidents, uncontrolled anger, dangerous conditions, and callousness are associated with this aspect. Military career persons frequently have this aspect.

Mars square Uranus

Death through accidents is a definite possibility with persons who have this aspect because they tend to be reckless, impulsive, and react suddenly without first exercising good judgment.

Mars square Neptune

Drug, alcohol, and sexual abuse are associated with this aspect. In heavily afflicted horoscopes there may be dishonesty or even criminal activity.

Mars square Pluto

This is a dangerous aspect because the person is inclined to use force to get whatever they want. In an otherwise good horoscope, it indicates great courage. These people are attracted to violent situations, such as wars, rebellions, riots, and often die a violent death.

Mars square Ascendant

These people may be bullies. They tend to be overly aggressive in their relationships with others.

Mars square Midheaven
There is generally strife both at work and at home, with problems at one place triggering problems at the other place. There is also a tendency to get into trouble with the law.

Jupiter square Saturn
There are difficulties or misfortunes in business and financial matters. Sometimes this is due to poor planning or poor judgment. Sometimes they lack confidence or fail to take the initiative at the right time.

Jupiter square Uranus
These are restless people who constantly seek adventure, often through travel. Usually they cannot be depended on to fulfill their promises, nor can their friends. They are usually Bohemian type people.

Jupiter square Neptune
These are skillful talkers whose words are meaningless because they never back them up with constructive action. They tend to be lazy and live in a dream world while their real world crumbles around them.

Jupiter square Pluto
These people don't hesitate to take the law into their own hands in order to change society to conform to their ideas. These usually are not nice or popular people.

Jupiter square Ascendant
Here you find the "holier than thou" people. They also tend to spread themselves too thin.

Jupiter square Midheaven
These people have grandiose ideas about their own

worth and their potential achievements. They need more humility and common sense.

Saturn square Uranus

These people vacillate between conservative and radical behavior. They tend to be dictators and are oppressive toward those who have different views than they have. Sudden misfortune may occur to them.

Saturn square Neptune

Fear of being inadequate and an inferiority complex go with this aspect. Others tend to shun these people because of their peculiar behavior. Various phobias are often connected with this aspect.

Saturn square Pluto

These people often feel that they are carrying the weight of the entire world on their shoulders because this aspect brings heavy responsibilities and many disappointments.

Saturn square Ascendant

These people are excluded from social activity because of their sour, cold, unresponsive disposition. They have difficulty in finding a marriage partner, and if they do the odds are overwhelmingly in favor of a divorce. They have few, if any, friends.

Saturn square Midheaven

They have to work extremely hard to care for their families because heavy burdens are always on their shoulders. Often their parents are a burden. Their life in general is filled with obstacles to happiness.

Uranus square Neptune

This square lasts for many years and is indicative of an entire generation. It usually is not prominent in individual charts unless Uranus or Neptune are quite strong in the chart. This tends to make individuals "set in their ways" and subject to nervousness; they are often "high strung."

Uranus square Pluto

This aspect lasts for years and is not prominent in individual charts unless Uranus or Pluto are otherwise strong in the chart. Individuals never feel secure no matter how much they have.

Uranus square Ascendant

These people are non-conformists to the extent that they create problems for themselves. They are prone to divorce because they are not willing to give up a little personal freedom in order to make the marriage work.

Uranus square Midheaven

These people refuse to conform to any routine. They rebel against authority—their boss, the government, parents. They change jobs and residences frequently for no valid reason. They have the "hippie" syndrome.

Neptune square Pluto

This rules corrupt social and governmental conditions for generations. There is no one alive today who has this aspect in their natal horoscope.

Neptune square Ascendant

This aspect denotes unreliable, deceptive, confused people who live in their own dream world.

Neptune square Midheaven

Unless the rest of the horoscope negates this influence, the person will be disorganized, unreliable, lazy, inefficient, and sometimes dishonest. One good aspect to Neptune from some other planet is usually sufficient to negate this aspect.

Pluto square Ascendant

A tendency for aggressive and antisocial behavior characterize this aspect. Divorce is almost a given, and there is high likelihood of lawsuits.

Pluto square Midheaven

These people want to change things to suit them, and they cause much conflict in the process. They tend to not get along very well with supervisors or authorities in general.

OPPOSITIONS

Sun opposition Moon

These people are born during the full Moon, which can give them difficulty in relationships with others. Due to stressful relationships, they can develop health problems, especially psychosomatic ailments or nervous conditions. If either the Sun or Moon has a trine to any other planet, it will greatly lessen the effect of this full Moon stigma.

Sun opposition Mars

These people are extremely difficult to get along with because they always want to argue or fight. Because they are continuously psyched up for doing battle, they eventually put a strain on their heart.

Sun opposition Jupiter

These people are much too optimistic. They promise much, but deliver little. Sometimes they are showoffs or are just plain arrogant.

Sun opposition Saturn

It is difficult for these people to develop friendships because they are too stiff and formal, even cold, in their demeanor. As a result, they usually marry late in life, if they even marry at all. Often they do not have children of their own.

Sun opposition Uranus

It is difficult for others to get along with these people because they insist on everything having to be done their way. They also tend to be irritable and tense, making others feel uncomfortable. They do crazy things for no good reason other than because they felt like doing them.

Sun opposition Neptune

This aspect bestows confusion and distorted understanding coupled with prejudices. Often they are deceitful or dishonest, and they tend to live in their own fantasy world.

Sun opposition Pluto

This is the classic dictator aspect—extremely overbearing, forceful will power that demands others to do what they want, and a desire to transform the world in accordance with their personal beliefs. Needless to say, these people's life is often in danger.

Moon opposition Mercury

These are prattling bores that everyone strives to avoid being around. They never shut up, and they never say anything worth listening to. They also cannot take criticism of any kind.

Moon opposition Venus
Sexual excesses and dietary excesses characterize this aspect. Domestic problems are common.

Moon opposition Mars
Alcoholism is common with this aspect. There often are temper outbursts over insignificant things that can be followed by violence. The men tend to treat women poorly, and the women tend to be unfeminine. They also tend to be irresponsible.

Moon opposition Jupiter
Extravagance in general, and overeating in particular, are associated with this aspect. They tend to be wasteful. They also are all talk and no action.

Moon opposition Saturn
Early childhood experience usually has a marked effect on these people, leaving them depressed, overly formal and unable to establish friendships. They have difficulty in getting along with employers (parental figures), thus creating conflicts at work which usually spill over to the domestic scene.

Moon opposition Uranus
Perversity, instability, undependability, unpredictability, sudden changes in mood, and irritability are marks of this aspect. Mothers neglect their children. Men neglect their wives.

Moon opposition Neptune
Alcohol and drug abuse are common with this as-

pect. Their domestic life is often in shambles due to irre-
sponsibility and laziness. Sometimes they get involved in
shady money making schemes.

Moon opposition Pluto
Intense emotions cause problems in relationships
with family and friends. There are sometimes family
quarrels concerning inheritance.

Mercury opposition Mars
These people are prone to argue at the drop of a hat,
which makes them unpopular. They are unable to see the
other person's point of view. They love to find fault with
others.

Mercury opposition Jupiter
These are daydreamers who talk big, but don't follow through. If they go to college, they will take some
course of study that has no practical value once they
graduate.

Mercury opposition Saturn
These are critical nags who see the dark side of everything. They tend to be narrow minded and highly opinionated. They are inclined to respiratory disorders; smok-
ing is especially harmful to them.

Mercury opposition Uranus
These people tend to be blunt and tactless, eccentric,
stubborn, arrogant and conceited. No one can make them
change their mind no matter what, but they may change
their mind of their own choice dozens of times a day.

Mercury opposition Neptune
Deceit and scheming are tendencies common with

this aspect.

Mercury opposition Pluto

These people often deal with secret or dangerous information, which causes them great mental tension and distress. Spying or detective work are sometimes associated with this aspect. In extreme cases, the nature of their work can bring about their death.

Venus opposition Mars

This aspect signifies emotional problems in relationships, often of a sexual nature. These people are easily hurt by other people's unkindness. This is not a favorable aspect for a good marriage.

Venus opposition Jupiter

Marital problems may occur over religious matters. Hypocrisy rears its head occasionally. These people have such a sickeningly sweet behavior that it irritates others.

Venus opposition Saturn

An unhappy marriage, financial hardships, and depression often accompany this aspect. There are all sorts of emotional frustrations that go with this aspect.

Venus opposition Uranus

Emotional instability is the keyword here. Many divorces are common. Many sudden, short lived romances are common. They foolishly squander money.

Venus opposition Neptune

Drug and alcohol abuse often enter the picture here. There may be scandals due to secret love affairs or other secret involvements. In some cases, there are homosexual tendencies.

Venus opposition Pluto

There are uncontrollable passions here that can cause many problems. They often attract undesirable associations into their life. Criminal involvement with sex, such as prostitution, in order to make money is sometimes present. Suicide attempts due to disappointment in love is a definite possibility.

Mars opposition Jupiter

This is the aspect of the soldier of fortune. Everything they do is self-serving. They are zealous in promoting their own religion or philosophy to the point of alienating others.

Mars opposition Saturn

These people are frustrated, and they use violent, aggressive action to cover-up their own fears and inadequacies in relation to others. Their own ambitions are often thwarted by others. In extreme cases, criminal tendencies may appear.

Mars opposition Uranus

There is danger of a violent death with this aspect. Bad temper is common. There is often involvement in dangerous or unstable situations. Friends often become enemies.

Mars opposition Neptune

Drugs and alcohol are dangerous for these people. They often take action without rational thought. Psychosomatic illness is fairly common.

Mars opposition Pluto

These people use power solely for selfish reasons. In extreme cases they resort to extreme violence. A violent death is common.

Jupiter opposition Saturn

Legal problems and lawsuits are probable with this aspect. There can also be difficulties in long distance travel and in foreign countries. These people are seldom happy, and are often under pressure to do more than they are capable of.

Jupiter opposition Uranus

Money gets frittered away in unwise "get rich quick" schemes. These people usually mean well, but they have no sense of reality. They will suddenly change courses or take off on trips with no rational reason.

Jupiter opposition Neptune

These people are generally unreliable and impractical. They do not fulfill their promises more due to forgetfulness than to deliberate dishonesty. Drugs, alcohol, gases and fumes pose a serious danger to them.

Jupiter opposition Pluto

There is conflict with others because these people have persistent determination to indoctrinate others with their religious and philosophic views. These people generally lack humility.

Saturn opposition Uranus

These people work hard, but have no common sense and are poor planners. They also preach one thing, but practice something else. Unexpected events constantly thwart their progress.

Saturn opposition Neptune

A persecution complex goes with this aspect. They

do not trust anyone. Sometimes they must be institution-alized or are plagued by hard to diagnose and cure psychological problems.

Saturn opposition Pluto

This aspect brings misfortune into the life. They can receive or give cruelty.

Uranus opposition Neptune

This long lasting aspect affects a generation of people. In individual horoscopes it can be involved with alcoholism, sexual involvements or excesses, or neurotic behavior.

Uranus opposition Pluto

This aspect indicates a generation of people whose lives are disrupted by social and political upheaval such as war or economic depression.

Neptune opposition Pluto

This aspect involves a generation of people. It is apparent in individual charts only if both planets are in angular houses and are heavily aspected by other planets, in which case they will behave in a manner quite different from their peers.

14

Signs on the House Cusps

Whatever zodiac sign appears on the cusp of a house rules that house. Each sign has certain basic attributes that influence the house it rules.

Each house has certain basic attributes of a person's life that it rules.

To interpret this interaction between the house and ruling sign, simply combine the attributes of both the house and its ruling sign. I'll give you an example at the end of this chapter.

The following are two tables of attributes, one for houses and one for signs, that you can use for a quick reference when interpreting natal charts.

Table 1

HOUSE ATTRIBUTES

(See Chapter 7 for more extensive detail)

First House	Your physical body and personality. How others perceive you. Self-awareness and self-interest. Life and health to some extent.
Second House	Income that you earn or acquire. Your money and possessions. Your material resources in general.
Third House	Your conscious mind and thought processes. Mental activity in general. Your brothers, sisters, and neighbors. Short distance travel and accidents during travel. Communications of all sorts.
Fourth House	Your home, both as a child and in adulthood when you have your own home. Domestic life in general. The end of any matter.
Fifth House	Romance. Love life. Sports. Gambling and speculation. Children. Entertainment and parties. Creative ability and creative urge.
Sixth House	Your health. Working conditions and tools. Clothing. Your employees. Service to others. Small animals.

House Attributes (Continued)

Seventh House	Marriage and other partnerships. Relations with others. Open enemies.
Eighth House	Death. Inheritance. Insurance. Taxes. Other people's money. Sexual matters. Investigations.
Ninth House	Religion or other philosophical beliefs. Foreign countries and foreign travel (long distance travel in general). Large animals. Publishing and printing. Law and legal matters. Educational matters. Dreams and some psychic experiences.
Tenth House	Your true profession in life. Ambitions. Public reputation. Social and professional status. Honors.
Eleventh House	Friends. Groups of people. Your wishes, hopes, and dreams. Your relationship with the government.
Twelfth House	Secrets. Hidden enemies. Self-delusion. Institutions of all sorts. Work and activity behind the scenes, out of the public eye. Some psychic matters such as seances.

Table 2

SIGN ATTRIBUTES

Aries	Action. Much energy. Impulsiveness. Combativeness. Leadership. Enthusiasm. Strife.
Taurus	Possessiveness. Profit. Slow but steady progress. Stubborness. Determination. Reliability. Slow to change. Dynamic when aroused.
Gemini	Much communication of all sorts. Much mental effort expended. Short distance travel. Diversity.
Cancer	Moodiness. Extreme sensitivity. Much intuition or psychic insight. Tenacity. Domestic matters. Association with food. Need for public recognition.
Leo	Pride. Enjoyment. Romance. Children. Optimism. Flamboyance. Tempermental reactions. Games, gambling, and speculation.
Virgo	Much discrimination. Caution. Analysis. Work. Perfectionism. Efficiency. Details. Craftsmanship. Critical and flaw seeking. Health. Service to others.

Sign Attributes (Continued)

Libra	Partnerships. Joint enterprises. Refinement. Harmony. Balance. Fairness. Beauty. Overly romantic or idealistic.
Scorpio	Secrecy. Vindictiveness. Coercion. Intense emotions and desires. Jealousy. Possessiveness. Sometimes meanness. Fatalistic attitude. Forced changes. Never gives up.
Sagittarius	Good fortune. Abundance. Optimism. Lack of discrimination. Foreign matters. Long distance travel. Philosophy. Humor.
Capricorn	Ambition. Self-discipline. Hard work. Responsibility. Desire for status. Seriousness. Frugality. Public ambitions. Business. Honors. Coldness.
Aquarius	Freedom. Independence. Unconventional. Humanitarian. Artistic talents. Friends. Sudden changes and events. Expensive tastes. Much originality. Inventiveness. Scientific and electrical methods.
Pisces	Sympathy. Understanding. Activities behind the scenes. Secretiveness. Fraud. Psychic matters. Institutions of all sorts. Sick people. Drugs.

Here is an example from figure 1 to illustrate how to interpret the sign influence on a house cusp. In figure 1, Virgo is on the second house cusp.

The second house pertains to how I will earn my money. Virgo defines the parameters of craftsmanship, details, service to others, work, perfectionism, analysis, flaw seeking, and efficiency. This means I will work at an occupation that employs these traits.

I am a professional writer, specializing in non-fiction, self-help, how-to books. All of the Virgo traits are absolutely necessary for success in earning money in this profession.

It all fits neatly, doesn't it? Play around with it in your own chart. It is an excellent way to learn astrology.

15

Putting It All Together

Now you have had your basic training in natal astrology. You know the language. You know how a natal chart is constructed. You have chapters of reference data to refer to in order to compile a natal chart interpretation that covers many salient facts.

All that remains now is for you to compile an interpretation. Here is how, using the natal chart in figure 1:

1. The 1st house cusp has Leo on it. Look up "Leo" and "First House" in Chapter 14 and write them down.

2. Neptune is in Leo in the 1st house. Look up "Neptune in Leo" in Chapter 11 and "Neptune in First House" in chapter 12 and write them down. Neptune is also conjunct the ascendant, conjunct Mars, trine Saturn, square Venus, and widely square Jupiter. Look up all of these aspects in Chapter 13 and write them down.

3. Proceed around the chart, house by house, planet by planet until you have written down all the interpretations.

4. Now read over all you have written. You will see patterns forming. For example, you will see (in this specific chart) that writing ability appears several times. Thus

you can conclude that the person (me in this case) is going to be, or should be, a professional writer. You will also see some things that cancel out other things. For example, the positive effects of Saturn trine Neptune cancel out or mitigate the negative effects of Venus square Neptune. Many things appear only once, and are not likely to apply to me, or if they do it would be only superficially.

5. Step 4 above enables you to synthesize the data into an accurate analysis of the natal chart.

In practice, you do not have to start your interpretation at the 1st house and proceed systematically around the chart as I have done in the preceding example. You can start anywhere, jump around, whatever, just as long as you eventually cover everything. It all comes out the same in the end.

As you become more experienced and have more data committed to memory, you will see major natal patterns and meanings in an instant without having to look everything up.

When I first look at a chart, I note the patterning first. How many planets are on the east side (left half), how many on the west side (right half), how many in the top half and how many in the bottom half? What planets are they? How are they clustered? This only takes seconds, and it tells me a great deal before I even start looking at specific detail.

Let me digress briefly to discuss patterning a little. Patterning really is an advanced astrology study, but I want to at least familiarize you with it.

At a quick glance, the astrologer notices where all the planets are. Here are some rules of thumb that the astrologer notices:

How many planets are in angular houses (houses 1, 4, 7, and 10) ? If the majority of planets are in angular houses, it indicates a prominent position in the world.

How many planets are in succedent houses (houses 2, 5, 8, and 11)? If the majority of planets are in succedent houses, it may make the person stubborn and uncompromising.

How many planets are in cadent houses (houses 3, 6, 9, and 12)? If the majority of the planets are in cadent houses, the person will probably complete a major part of some undertaking, but someone else will get credit for it.

If the majority of the planets are in the left half of the chart, it indicates a leadership ability. If the majority are in the right half, it indicates a person who would rather not lead if they can avoid it.

If the majority of the planets are in the bottom half of the chart, the person most likely goes through life reacting to outside stimuli for direction. If the majority are in the top half, the person chooses his/her own direction rather than being directed by outside stimuli.

The majority in cardinal signs indicates a self-starter; in mutable signs, a thinker or intellectual; in fixed signs, a person who can get things done when they have a direction given to them.

Whenever there is a cluster of four or more planets it is a flag that something unusual, extreme, or outstanding will take place in the person's life.

And there is much more to patterning than what I have just given. The astrologer can mentally blend the nearly infinite number of patterns into a reasonably clear picture before actually studying each facet of the chart in detail.

Look at figure 1 for the patterning. Eight of the ten planets are on the left side of the chart. I have been a non-commissioned officer in the military and an executive with IBM. The leadership firs the patterning, does it not?

Seven of the ten planets are in the top half of the chart. I am extremely independent, and I make things happen for myself; I never wait for something external to happen to determine what I will do. It fits again.

Notice the cluster of four planets in the 10th house in figure 1. With the particular planets involved, it assures the person of a prominent place in the world and public recognition. I have a number of books published domestically and internationally, which brings me considerable recognition. Again it all fits.

What I have given merely scratches the surface of patterning. I have had to make a judgment call on what to leave out of this book so it wouldn't be so huge that it would intimidate the beginner and so expensive that very few people would purchase it.

By the same token, I have given only some of the salient data for each sign, planet, house, and aspect. There is sufficient material in this book to satisfy most of you, let you have fun, and also learn a great deal about yourself and other people.

In Part IV, I list some references for those of you who want to take the next step and learn more and do more with astrology.

Astrology is one pursuit that is fun, gives mental stimulation, provides valuable knowledge and insights, is relatively easy to learn, can soak up as much time as you are able to give it, and it sets you apart as a unique individual. One thing—you never learn it all, so it is always a challenge.

Now get busy and have a good time in the world of astrology!

16

Transits and Progressions

We all would like to be able to look into the future to see what potentially lies in store for us. When is a favorable time to do something, such as getting married, signing a contract, seeking a different job, etc.? When is an unfavorable time to do these things?

Well, you can look into your future using your natal chart. This is what transits and progressions are all about - predictive astrology. The subject is easily an entire book by itself and is beyond the scope of "beginner." I mention this subject of predictive astrology to you as a recommendation for your next step of study. It is exciting and valuable. Now that you know the basics, you will be able to master predictive astrology quite easily.

In brief, predictive astrology deals with the planetary movements and positions at any given time in the future as it relates to your natal chart.

As a hypothetical example, assume that on July 18, 1999 transiting Uranus becomes trine your natal Sun and sextile your natal Pluto. This could trigger an era of psychic awareness and experience for you that would change your entire life.

Enough said. If you are interested in the future, explore predictive astrology.

PART IV

REFERENCE MATERIAL

17

References

This chapter contains information concerning organizations, books, and other material that can help you expand your own astrological horizons in whatever direction you choose. I do not imply that the data in this chapter is all there is or that other sources (not listed) might not be just as good.

What I have put in this chapter concerns sources that I am personally familiar with and that I feel comfortable in recommending to you at this stage of your learning experience.

I have not put the information in any particular order and the item number does not indicate any preference over another item lower in this list. This is simply a discussion of some sources for your consideration. It is sort of a "jump start" for your further expansion into astrology.

1. Llewellyn Publications. This publisher has an expansive line of astrology books, services, and materials. I especially recommend: (a) Their computerized natal chart service, which is very reasonably priced; (b) Their several astrological calendars, which contain a wealth of astrology information in addition to being a calendar; (c) Their

Daily Planetary Guide, which is filled with great information and features.

They offer a great deal more. I recommend you write or phone them (toll free) to request a free copy of their catalog and a list of all their astrology books, services, and materials. Here is how to contact Llewellyn:

> **Llewellyn Publications**
> P.O. Box 64383-307
> St. Paul, MN 55164-0383
> Phone (toll free): 1-800-THE-MOON

2. Your local bookstore that specializes in astrology books. Browse through the astrology section.

3. Your local library. This is where I spent hundreds of hours in the beginning. They should have an ephemeris, tables of houses, and a wide variety of astrology books.

4. Evangeline Adams. This great astrologer is now deceased, but she left a legacy of excellent books. Read everything you can by her. She is probably one of the finest astrologers of all time. You may have difficulty finding her books through a bookstore, but the library should have them.

5. The American Federation of Astrologers. This is an excellent professional association of which I am a member. They offer associate memberships to beginners and have an extensive list of books, materials, and services available to members. Their annual dues are quite reasonable. If this interests you, you can write for information on joining to:

> **American Federation of Astrologers**
> P.O. Box 22040
> Tempe, Arizona 85282

6. Computer programs for astrology. If you have a

computer, or are considering buying one, and want to obtain the required software, you can write to:

Matrix Software
315 Marion Avenue
Big Rapids, Michigan 49307
Or phone: (616) 796-2483

I have had Matrix software for years and use it frequently. I find it to be excellent. Before you purchase a computer and printer, write to Matrix to find out which computers and printers are compatible with their software. This will prevent you from purchasing equipment that won't work.

7. Predictive astrology. This is what I talked about very briefly in Chapter 16. An excellent book on this subject is *Predictive Astrology* by Frances Sakoian and Louis S. Acker, published by Harper & Row.

8. Sun Signs. There are several excellent books on Sun Signs. Query Llewellyn Publications about their offerings (see above for address and phone number). In addition, Evangeline Adams, mentioned in item #4 above, wrote an excellent one. Another excellent one is *Linda Goodman's Sun Signs* by Linda Goodman, published by Bantam Books in paperback.

9. Degrees. Each degree in the horoscope wheel has a specific significance. For an interpretation of the degrees, I especially like *Practical Astrology: How to Make it Work For You* by Jerryl L. Keane, published by Parker Publishing Company. This book also contains other astrology information, but I use it exclusively for reference on degree interpretation.

10. An all around good reference for chart interpretation is *The Astrologer's Handbook* by Frances Sakoian & Louis S. Acker, which covers interpretation on a more ex-

panded scale.

11. Transits. An excellent companion book for the one mentioned in #7 above is *Transits Simplified* by Frances Sakoian and Louis Acker, published by Harper & Row. By now you must be aware that Frances Sakoian and Louis Acker are prominent astrologers.

12. Ephemeris. There are a number of ephemerides books on the market, and they all are pretty much the same—all are good. The two I happen to have are: *The Concise Planetary Ephemeris for 1900 to 1950 A.D. at Midnight* and *The Complete Planetary Ephemeris 1950-2000 A.D.*, which is also a midnight ephemeris. Both are published by The Hieratic Publishing Co.

13. Tables of Houses. There are many tables of houses on the market, and they are all good and all pretty much the same. The one I happen to have is *The American Book of Tables*, published by Astro Computing Services.

14. Time changes. I recommend *Time Changes In The U.S.A.* by Doris Chase Doane, published by the American Federation of Astrologers, Inc. This book should be available through your bookstore. If not, write to the address in #5 above. Ms. Doane has also written other time changes books for Canada, Mexico, and the world. If you are going to compile natal charts for persons born outside the United States, you will want to get these other time changes books also.

☽ LOOK FOR THE CRESCENT MOON

Llewellyn publishes hundreds of books on your favorite subjects! To get these exciting books, including the ones on the following pages, check your local bookstore or order them directly from Llewellyn.

ORDER BY PHONE

- Call toll-free within the U.S. and Canada, 1-800-THE MOON
- In Minnesota, call (612) 291-1970
- We accept VISA, MasterCard, and American Express

ORDER BY MAIL

- Send the full price of your order (MN residents add 7% sales tax) in U.S. funds, plus postage & handling to:

    Llewellyn Worldwide
    P.O. Box 64383, Dept. L307-8
    St. Paul, MN 55164–0383, U.S.A.

POSTAGE & HANDLING

(For the U.S., Canada, and Mexico)

- $4.00 for orders $15.00 and under
- $5.00 for orders over $15.00
- No charge for orders over $100.00

We ship UPS in the continental United States. We ship standard mail to P.O. boxes. Orders shipped to Alaska, Hawaii, The Virgin Islands, and Puerto Rico are sent first-class mail. Orders shipped to Canada and Mexico are sent surface mail.

International orders: Airmail—add freight equal to price of each book to the total price of order, plus $5.00 for each non-book item (audio tapes, etc.).

Surface mail—Add $1.00 per item.

Allow 4–6 weeks for delivery on all orders.
Postage and handling rates subject to change.

DISCOUNTS

We offer a 20% discount to group leaders or agents. You must order a minimum of 5 copies of the same book to get our special quantity price.

FREE CATALOG

Get a free copy of our color catalog, *New Worlds of Mind and Spirit*. Subscribe for just $10.00 in the United States and Canada ($30.00 overseas, airmail). Many bookstores carry *New Worlds*—ask for it!

Visit our web site at www.llewellyn.com for more information.

HEAVEN KNOWS WHAT
Grant Lewi

Here's the fun, new edition of the classic, *Heaven Knows What!*
What better way to begin the study of astrology than to actually do it while you learn. *Heaven Knows What* contains everything you need to cast and interpret complete natal charts
without memorizing any symbols, without confusing calculations, and without previous experience or training. The
tear-out horoscope blanks and special "aspect wheel" make it
amazingly easy.

The author explains the influence of every natal Sun and
Moon combination, and describes the effects of every major
planetary aspect in language designed for the modern reader.
His readable and witty interpretations are so relevant that
even long- practicing astrologers gain new psychological
insight into the characteristics of the signs and meanings of
the aspects.

Grant Lewi is sometimes called the father of "do-it-yourself" astrology, and is considered by many to have been
astrology's forerunner to the computer.

0-87542-444-9
480 pp., 6 x 9, tables, charts, softcover $14.95

THE INSTANT HOROSCOPE READER
Planets by Sign, House and Aspect
Julia Lupton Skalka

Find out what was written in the planets at your birth! Almost everyone enjoys reading the popular Sun sign horoscopes in newspapers and magazines; however, there is much more to astrology than knowing what your Sun sign is. How do you interpret your natal chart so that you know what it means to have Gemini on your 8th house cusp? What does astrology say about someone whose Sun is conjoined with natal Jupiter?

The Instant Horoscope Reader was written to answer such questions and to give beginners a fresh, thorough overview of the natal chart. Here you will find the meaning of the placement of the Sun, the Moon and each planet in the horoscope, including aspects between the natal planets, the meaning of the houses in the horoscope and house rulerships. Even if you have not had your chart cast, this book includes simple tables that enable you to locate the approximate planetary and house placements and figure the planetary aspects for your birthdate to give you unique perspectives about yourself and others.

1-56718-669-6
6 x 9, 272 pp., illus.

$14.95

**INSTANT HOROSCOPE
PREDICTOR**
Find Your Future Fast
Julia Lupton Skalka

Want to know if the planets will smile favorably upon your wedding day? Wondering when to move ahead on that new business venture? Perhaps you're curious as to why you've been so accident prone lately. It's time to look at your transits.

Transits define the relationship between where the planets are today with where they were when you were born. They are an invaluable aid for timing your actions and making decisions. With a copy of your transit chart (easily available from any astrological computing service) and the book *Instant Horoscope Predictor*, you can now discover what's in store for today, next month, even a year from now. Julia Lupton Skalka delivers an easy-to-use guide that will decipher the symbols on your transit chart into clear, usable predictions. In addition, she provides chapters on astrological history, mythology, and transit analyses of four famous people: Grace Kelly, Mata Hari, Theodore Roosevelt and Ted Bundy.

1-56718-668-8
 6 x 9, 464 pp., softcover   **$14.95**

MEET YOUR PLANETS
Fun with Astrology
Roy Alexander

Astrology doesn't have to be mind boggling. Now there is a playful way to master this ancient art! In this book, the planets are transformed into an unforgettable lot of characters with very distinctive personalities and idiosyncrasies. Maybe you're the Temple Dancer, a temptress oozing with exotic flair... the Tennis Champion, with his win-at-all-costs attitude ... or maybe the Math Teacher, an unrelenting stickler for proof and accuracy. Furthermore, the twelve signs of the zodiac are turned into 9-to-5 jobs; if a planet doesn't like its job, it will complain, procrastinate, throw a temper tantrum—typical human behavior. Now you can relate to the planets as people you know, work and play with. Finally, astrology doesn't take itself so seriously! You'll be amazed at how easy and fun learning the art of astrology is ... seriously!

1-56718-017-5
224 pp., 6 x 9, 142 illus., softcover   **$12.95**

MYTHIC ASTROLOGY
Archetypal Powers in the Horoscope
Ariel Guttman &
Kenneth Johnson

Here is an entirely new dimension of self-discovery based on understanding the mythic archetypes represented in the astrological birth chart. Myth has always been closely linked with astrology; all our planets are named for the Graeco-Roman deities and derive their interpretative meanings from them. To richly experience the myths which lie at the heart of astrology is to gain a deeper and more spiritual perspective on the art of astrology and on life itself.

Mythic Astrology is unique because it allows the reader to explore the connection between astrology and the spirituality of myth in depth, without the necessity of a background in astrology, anthropology or the classics. This book is an important contribution to the continuing study of mythology as a form of New Age spirituality and is also a reference work of enduring value. Students of mythology, the Goddess, art, history, Jungian psychological symbolism and literature—as well as lovers of astrology—will all enjoy the text and numerous illustrations.

0-87542-248-9
382 pp., 7 x 10, 100 illus., softcover $17.95

THE CELTIC LUNAR ZODIAC
How to Interpret Your Moon Sign
Helena Paterson, illustrated by
Margaret Walty

The people of Celtic Europe have watched the skies for centuries, developing their astrology into a precise and sophisticated science. To them, the movement of the Moon was just as important as the movement of the Sun because it helped to round out the picture of the personality. For further clarification, they also related the thirteen lunar months of the year to specific trees, flowers and gemstones.

Our ancestors recognized the intimate relationship between the movements of the stars and the natural world. Now, Helena Paterson offers you a treasure trove of insights into Celtic mythology, herbal lore and Druidic mystery tradition. Clearly presented and beautifully illustrated with Margaret Walty's symbolic watercolors, *The Celtic Lunar Zodiac* opens up an enticing new dimension into astrological interpretation.

1-56718-510-X
9 x 9, 160 pp., color illus. $17.95

To order, call 1-800-THE MOON
Prices subject to change without notice